The
Terminal
Generation

The Terminal Generation

by Hal Lindsey

with C. C. Carlson

FLEMING H. REVELL COMPANY
Old Tappan, New Jersey

Library of Congress Cataloging in Publication Data

Lindsey, Hal.
    The terminal generation.

    Includes bibliographical references.
    1. Hope. I. Carlson, Carole C., joint author.
II. Title.
BV4638.L56   234'.2   76-14925
ISBN 0-8007-0794-X
ISBN 0-8007-0795-8 pbk.

TO

the families of the Lindseys and the Carlsons—whose love,
encouragement, and support were invaluable during the
writing of this book.

TO

Sally Johnson and John Weldon who contributed to the
research.

TO

the dear friends who prayed, laughed, and cried during the
birth of a book.

Contents

Introduction

This is a book about hope! If the title seems to deny this fact, it's no accident. *The Terminal Generation* is realistic. The promise of hope is factual.

There is nothing more essential to life than hope; without it a man may be breathing, but he's dead.

When we look around us we see a generation being engulfed in an accelerating crescendo of despair. The symptoms are everywhere. Perhaps they're even in you.

Because man can't live without hope, he is grasping for things which he thinks might give him direction, might provide the happiness he craves.

He grasps and slips, reaches and falls. Somewhere, somehow, that illusive ray must be found. Where?

Hope must be solid. Hope must be placed in something that is able to fulfill your expectations.

Here is the great danger of our times: As it is increasingly being driven toward pessimism and despair, this generation may become prey to a great hoax—to an infamous false hope that has been predicted in the Bible.

We stand on the precipice of both the greatest peril and the greatest realization of hope in the history of man.

A wrong choice today may be *terminal.*

The peril and the hope are present with us. Right now. As the peril increases, the hope becomes acutely essential.

It's my desire that this book may carry you—no matter whether you are negatively or positively charged, or somewhere in between —into an exciting new dimension of life-changing hope!

HAL LINDSEY

Man can live about 40 days without food, about 3 days without water, about 8 minutes without air . . . but only about 1 second without HOPE.

Those who know how close the connection is between the state of mind of a man—his courage and hope, or lack of them—will understand that the sudden loss of hope and courage can have a deadly effect.

VIKTOR FRANKL
Professor of Psychiatry, University of Vienna,
from his *Man's Search for Meaning*

1

The Dark Side of the Mood

Shalom resounded through our house as we welcomed people who were arriving for the party. Strains of Israeli folk music from the stereo provided the background for lox, bagels, and laughter in our crowded living room.

We were excited, anticipating a trip together to the Holy Land. The conversation vibrated with questions and plans. For most of our new friends this was a once-in-a-lifetime adventure, a dream tour into the Promised Land.

As we dimmed the lights and began to show a film of one of our former trips, we had a chance to observe the group. We had led tours before and knew that soon the members would become one big family. What would our new family be like? The generation span went from kindergarten, a troop of preteens, the in-betweens, to grandparents. What a great opportunity there would be for everyone to share common experiences from varied perspectives!

I found myself watching one man in particular. He sat on the couch, shifting position restlessly as we explained some of the details of our forthcoming travels. His thin fingers were never still; palms together, he flexed and unflexed his knuckles nervously. From time to time he jumped up and paced through the hall. It was his eyes that drew me; they were troubled and disturbed, haunted by some unknown force.

This man appeared on the brink of despair, although from the viewpoint of outsiders he had everything: a lovely and devoted wife, two bright and attractive teenagers, and an enormously successful business. I soon found out that Ted was a wealthy man, with a continuing income which could give him lifetime economic security. Why, I wondered, did he seem so depressed and restless?

We went on that trip to the Middle East, resulting in many astounding changes in some persons. Ted was one who returned with a new perspective on life.

A year later Ted finally asked me the question which had

bothered him for many months. "Hal, what did you see in me that night of the tour party? You kept staring at me."

"Ted, I saw the look of a man I once was—a man filled with confusion and hopelessness."

Ted's story is not isolated. A mental health expert reported, "About 100 million people—or 3% of the world's population—may be victims of nervous depression." [1]

THE WORRY EPIDEMIC

Stress is everywhere. It's not the exclusive trait of the affluent. In fact, during times of economic fear, it's the guy who is struggling to make the size of his paycheck meet the length of the month who is most subject to those extreme results of stress: mental illness, alcoholism, and suicide. At Johns Hopkins University, for instance, there was a study done on how economic changes—particularly recessions—lead to an increase in mental disorder.

A report from a Florida suicide-prevention center said: "We are getting a lot more self-injury and suicide behavior based on economic crises. The callers are often people who are not able to meet their monthly bills, who are losing their jobs for the first time and are panicked because economic failure is staring them in the face. Not all those who threaten or attempt suicide really want to die . . . they're really crying, 'Help me!'" [2]

Help me! It's the cry of those without hope.

A man wrote me his frank story:

I was in a state of spiritual nothingness and ready to end it all . . . I had 7 years of suffering, I couldn't hold a job, I had lost interest in everything, bills were piling up, everything. In 1964 I had been discharged from the army as a schizophrenic and thinking about this left me almost paralyzed. They told me there is no cure for schizophrenia and that mental hospital beds are full of them.

This story might have ended as a case history stamped DECEASED: CAUSE, SUICIDE but it didn't. Instead he found the hope he needed for survival and lived to write me of this vital discovery.

WHAT IS RIGHT AND WRONG?

Men depressed. Women searching. Children lost. Why are so many confused? Isn't there anything solid in this sea of shifting values?

People who study human behavior are arriving at conclusions about the change in our society. It's difficult for anyone to ignore the upheavals which have occurred in the past ten or fifteen years. Our shock systems have been overworked in the wide-open '70s.

For instance, a national news magazine had a feature article entitled "What's Happening to American Morality?" The answers came—not from churchmen—but from the sociologists and psychologists who present a studied and clinical analysis.

> . . . many sociologists and other delvers into modern morality conclude [that] a tidal wave of changing standards is creating widespread moral bewilderment, concern and resentment.
>
> Prof. Daniel Freedman, chairman of the department of psychiatry at the University of Chicago, reports: "Our society and this 'openness' have created adjustment problems for the individual. There are fewer of these problems when a society has widely accepted standards for morals and manners. Today, we don't have such a situation. This is a burden on the individual who, more than ever before, must make his or her own decisions as to what is right or wrong." [3]

That is the question: to be right or to be wrong. Who knows the standard? Many normally decent people are finding that it is easier to conform than it is to reform. Like an automobile without brakes on a mountain road, the perplexity of parents accelerates into the muddled minds of their children.

Here is what one child psychologist commented:

> Because many adults cannot handle sin, they remove the "sinful" stigma of an act, setting up new values to which they can con-

form—new standards for themselves, but none for children . . .
It will be difficult for these children in their adult lives to be
decision-makers about right and wrong, because without guidelines, they will have no idea what moral concepts are all about.[4]

Children without guidelines. This is one of the great tragedies
of our time. When children find themselves confused by conflicting standards they sometimes try to establish their own. I had a
letter from one young woman who told me of her search for
guidelines after her parents were divorced. She wrote:

> I rejected God when my parents were divorced . . . then I
> rejected every person who would try to direct me . . . all the
> time knowing inside of me there was a director. I wanted to see
> what was so evil about evil, what was so wrong about what others
> said was wrong . . . to find my way. I rebelled, turning on my
> parents first. I went through drugs, hallucinations, uppers and
> downers, moral degradation . . . all of the things people are
> shocked about when I speak of them.
> I didn't see until recently that through all the trials I had I was
> praying, "Dear Lord, Dear God, please help me!"

HELP ME!

This generation of children has followed the Peter Pan of per-
missiveness into a Never-Never Land which leads to nowhere.
A few years ago a collective sign seemed to lull parents and school
authorities into thinking that the worst epidemic of drugs was
over. The consensus seemed to be, "The kids have had their
fling . . . they're becoming more aware of the dangers of the
consequences."

Look at Haight-Ashbury, for instance. It has ceased to be the
Mecca for runaways long ago. Many prominent people today
openly confess they have smoked pot and thought it was harmless.

It's true. The iceberg of drugs has surfaced, but the treachery
remains beneath the waves.

In a government report it was told that there is a growing use
of marijuana among the very, very young. A George Washington
University researcher said, "The trend toward earlier introduction
to drug use is definitely upward."

This study stated that "marijuana use among 12–17 year olds almost doubled between 1972 and 1974." Dr. Robert L. DuPont, director of the National Institute of Drug Abuse, said, "It is apparently inevitable that young people are going to experiment with cigarettes, alcohol and marijuana, and that this experience will lead too many young people to a regular pattern of undesirable use of these drugs." [5]

What are the consequences? It means that children are left without an answer to their cry, "Help me!" It means that increasingly the young adults will be floundering without direction in a time when they should be building a family foundation.

And the family begins to crumble. From a small town in what used to be the solid core of America, a young woman wrote me this letter:

> Let me explain. At the ripe old age of 24 I was miserable. I thought love and romance were the key to a woman's happiness. There didn't seem to be any love in the world. Every time I reached out to someone I was either used or rejected. My husband was never home, and I began to look for fulfillment outside my marriage. I was like a puzzle with a piece missing.
>
> I went to a TM meeting, but they only seemed interested in your money. I also dabbled in astrology. I thought it was quite profound. At the same time I read *Chariots of the Gods*. I thought I had found some "truths" that made sense, and would help me get my head together.
>
> I ran around telling everyone about the new truth. There is no God, just men from other planets!

This young woman continued with her story of a nearly wrecked marriage. However, she had a complete reversal in her direction, which is another story where hope was found before it was too late.

WHERE DOES IT END?

What is the logical, wasteful conclusion for a human being in despair? Escape. The roads of escape are many. One of the oldest methods of personal oblivion is alcohol. Today we are discovering that more and more young people are imbibing. A report by the

National Institute on Alcohol Abuse and Alcoholism (NIAAA) claimed that 14 percent of the high-school seniors all over the USA became intoxicated at least once weekly. To this astounding statistic was added the fact, revealed by the U.S. Department of Health, Education, and Welfare, that by the seventh grade 63 percent of the boys and 54 percent of the girls in elementary school have taken at least one drink.[6]

Alcohol, according to Dr. Morris E. Chafetz, director of the NIAAA, is a factor in half of the homicides and one-third of the suicides all over the country.[6a]

Alcohol itself is not the root problem. It is particularly dangerous to one who has other basic emotional disturbances and needs to fill the emptiness of despair with the escape that alcohol offers.

Illustrations of the results of alcoholism surround us. The toll it has taken in the area where I live is sometimes more dramatic, simply because of the entertainment industry.

A woman who had once been a beautiful actress was admitted to a local hospital after one of her many suicide attempts. She was a familiar, but pathetic figure to the nurses. Her chiseled features, distorted and puffy, were the results of her own search for meaning.

Such emptiness of purpose—such despair in a world where beauty, money, and fame are envied by those on the outside of the world of make-believe! This actress plunged into one experience after another, resulting in broken lives and shattered hopes.

From the examples of Ted (our depressed friend at the tour party), the army veteran in economic despair, the woman who rejected everyone, the miserable young wife, the alcoholic actress, and thousands of letters I've received, I can see the despair rushing in like a tidal wave.

Maybe you don't see yourself in any of these examples; perhaps your distress button takes another form. What is it? Lack of purpose? Money problems? A marriage on the edge of destruction? Kids who have broken your heart—or parents who don't seem to care? Whatever . . . .

There is a desperate need for hope!

The Worldly Hope men set their Hearts upon Turns [to] Ashes.
OMAR KHAYYÁM

2

No Wonder

How ready are we to meet and combat this growing dark mood? Is the mettle of our characters made to withstand the impact of today's tornados?

Many lives are being affected by crumbling values. Many people are being ripped apart under stress because their basic fiber was made out of faulty material. As parents, husbands, wives, pastors, and friends look on, many say, "I wonder why Jim did that?" Or, "I wonder what happened to Pat!"

I wonder. Take Jim, for instance. He was quite a guy. In high school he was the star quarterback and everyone knew that the college scouts were watching him. His mother clipped all the articles about him from the local sports pages and pasted them in his scrapbook. She was so proud of him.

It wasn't just that Jim was an athlete. He was an honor student and class officer—a regular churchgoer, too. A lot was expected of him. When he got a scholarship to a top university it wasn't much of a surprise to anyone.

College was really big time for Jim. He wasn't sure of what he wanted to be, so he enrolled in a general liberal arts course, heavy on psychology and philosophy. He even took "The Bible as Literature" because he thought it would be a snap.

A couple of semesters went by and Jim began to think there were many dimensions to life he had never known. His church, for instance, was really out of it. His parents were great people, of course, but their way of living was too materialistic. All they thought about was work, make the payments on a house, and gripe about inflation. Not for him. He had discovered a new freedom of thought. He began to wonder why he was here—if work and achievement were the only important goals.

That course on the Bible really opened his eyes. He had always heard that the Bible was the final authority. He really couldn't swallow that. It was okay for uneducated people, but he learned from the professor that there were too many inconsistencies in it for him.

Gradually he began to discard the old standards for a new, freer way of thinking. Jim's life-style became more consistent with his changed philosophy as he began to smoke pot and got into stronger drugs. Grades began to drag; he dropped off the football team, and pretty soon nothing seemed too important except the weekend parties in the apartment he shared with his girl friend.

Then there was Linda. Her background wasn't pretty. Divorced parents, growing up with mixed loyalties between a mom who really tried to make a decent life for her, and a weekend father who gave her flashes of excitement in a dreary existence. Then the weekends became less frequent (he was so busy), and by the time Linda was in her teens life was an empty house after school, a tired mother with a succession of men friends, and an uncontrollable passion for food. Linda was sixteen and miserable. Her self-image was rotten. One night she went shopping and met someone who told her about this great "church" where everyone was welcome. Why not try it?

Before long Linda found the family she needed. This dynamic man from Korea had challenging ideas, a real purpose to offer. She packed her suitcase, left her mother a note, and joined the Unification Church. She thought that she had found a true cause, a real reason for living.

Some might say that Jim and Linda are young—they'll get their values straightened out after a while. But then we meet someone like Pat, the attractive mother of two preteens, wife of a computer salesman. Pat spent a lot of time during the day reading women's magazines and watching television. She was bored and restless, dissatisfied with herself and tired of suburbia.

One day Pat's husband came home and found the note. "I'm sick of everything. You and the kids don't really need me anymore —I need to find myself—I need just to be me. Don't try to talk me into coming back." She joined the growing army of so-called liberated women.

These are real-life examples of people touched by a new look at old standards.

What's happening? A universal cry of concerned people everywhere is "Where did we go wrong?" One of America's national magazines said, "Great shifts are occurring in the way people look at such basic values as freedom, justice, ambition and excellence." [7]

Great shifts have occurred in the past century—shifts which have now developed into such earthquake proportions that we are caught in an avalanche of disintegrating values. Why? What started the tremors which began in the nineteenth century and have proceeded to shake our foundations in the twentieth century?

PHILOSOPHY, PROPHECY, AND YOU

Events and ideas which mold our lives are like the genes which determine the color of our eyes. We can't see the ideas or the genes, but we live with the results.

I believe that a certain elite group of philosophic thinkers has established thought patterns which affect every facet of our lives today. Philosophy is not abstract; it is not an obscure subject promoted by the ivory-tower intelligentsia in a manner the average person can't comprehend. Philosophy is the basis for the direction of the society we live in.

The philosophical grandfather who bred the ideas which fostered so many of our present thought forms was Hegel. This German advanced the idea that no truth exists, only opposite views or forces (thesis and antithesis) which come into conflict and then merge into a new force (synthesis) which itself becomes the new thesis.

The process of Hegelian conflict is constant. There is nothing absolute here, because everything is relative. This theory has provided the basis for the Western philosophies of pragmatism, humanism, scientism, and existentialism. These are the philosophies which now control education.

As Hegel's relative thinking marched into the universities and cultural centers of Europe, its philosophy exploded into the flood of ideas which eroded belief in absolute truth and morality.

Among Hegel's believers were some important men whose influence was widespread.

In a perceptive analysis one writer said: "Prophetic voices in the nineteenth century had been raised to proclaim the coming condition of modern man. Among these numerous voices were three that prove unforgettable: Marx, Kierkegaard and Nietzsche. The three thinkers saw the onrushing developments with peculiar clarity, and exert a magnetic influence on the beliefs of our own day." [8]

We should certainly include Darwin and Freud as spokesmen for the views which have spilled into every area. The threads which these men, and a few others who are lesser known, have woven have formed the net in which mankind is entangled today.

Philosophy is a world view; no one can live without having developed an attitude about himself and the world he lives in, whether he is conscious of it or not. Philosophy and religion both deal with the same basic question: man and his dilemma.

There are really four great questions of life. If we are to understand what is happening today, we need to examine what certain influential voices had to say about these questions.

Where did I come from?
Who am I?
Why am I here?
Where am I going?

WHERE DID I COME FROM?

In ancient times philosophers recognized a moral universe. There were standards which had an absolute basis. When Socrates and his Greek world were young, he hoped that the world of human affairs might be brought within the realm of universal reason. He believed that it was his moral duty to live in a moral world.

Plato followed along with this idea of morality on an absolute scale. He said in his *Dialogues*, ". . . a man who is good for anything . . . ought only to consider whether in doing anything he is doing right or wrong." [9]

These old philosophers saw right and wrong but their eighteenth-, nineteenth-, and twentieth-century counterparts changed those basic concepts completely and have held the view that there is no truth.

Let's begin with the question *Where did I come from?* The mind-molders of modern man believe that we spring from an impersonal beginning.

Here are a few quotes from the chain of thought which evolves from Darwin's Theory of Evolution. These are man's conclusions when he rejects God and tries to build a world view without Him.

Jacques Monod, French Nobel Prize winner in the field of physiology, said, ". . . chance alone is at the source of every innovation, of all creation in the biosphere. Pure chance, absolutely free but blind, [is] at the very root of the stupendous edifice of evolution." [10]

Jean Paul Sartre, influential philosopher, novelist and playwright of our time, wrote: "Every existence is born without reason, prolongs itself out of weakness and dies by chance." [11]

Bertrand Russell, the English atheist mathematician-philosopher with strong pacifist views, said, ". . . man . . . his origin, his growth, his hopes and fears, his loves and his beliefs, are but the outcome of accidental collocations of atoms; no fire, no heroism, no intensity of thought and feeling, can preserve an individual life beyond the grave . . . ." [12]

If what these men have said has any validity, if our creation was by chance, our existence without reason, and our identity an uncertainty, then we are led to examine the second great question of life: *Who am I?*

WHO AM I?

The vagrant sitting on a park bench, staring vacantly at the pigeons, doesn't stop to consider who he is, because he already believes he is nothing. The lonely kid thumbing a ride somewhere, just because it might offer something better than what he's known, unconsciously longs to have an identity—to be someone. He wonders, *Who am I?* The homemaker, occupied with what seems to be an endless routine—the factory worker fitting together electronic parts—the executive with the daily pressure of meetings and decisions—all need to know the answer to that fundamental question.

How have some of the influential philosophic thinkers explained man's personal identity?

Jean Paul Sartre: "First of all, man exists, turns up, appears on the scene, and only afterwards, defines himself. If man, as the existentialist conceives him is indefinable, it is because at first he is nothing." [13]

If man is nothing, as Sartre describes him, there are others who have similar views. Albert Camus, French philosopher and novelist, another Nobel Prize winner, wrote eloquently about man as he saw him. "The metaphysical rebel protests against the condition in which he finds himself as a man . . . the metaphysical rebel declares he is frustrated by the universe." [14]

The man who is "nothing," whose self-image is based upon his personal frustration, is a man without an anchor. As Camus explained, he saw himself as someone who could manage his life without any absolute values. He wrote: "Man can master in himself everything that should be mastered." [14a]

We are all programmed by the past. Soren Kierkegaard, a Danish philosopher who died more than 100 years ago, is growing in popularity in the United States in our time. His works, which were largely ignored during his lifetime, have become known a generation later in the existentialist line of thinking. The Existentialists found few solutions to basic problems, but they all agreed that mankind is alienated from a God who may or may not exist. Kierkegaard said that to be free man must choose himself, not God. He wrote: "Man left to himself has no spiritual recourse other than an absurd leap of faith into a blind unknown." [15]

What could we conclude from Kierkegaard's reasoning? Simply this: If we are alienated from a God (who may not even exist) we will find ourselves, in Kierkegaard's own words, in "fear and trembling." We are helpless victims of ignorance and dread. We are nothing! What a sad state of nonexistence.

Francis Schaeffer said this in describing the results of the teachings of such men as Sartre, Camus, Kierkegaard, and others: "He [meaning man] has no universals to cover the particulars in his own life. He is one thing inside and another thing outside. Then he begins to scream, 'Who am I?' . . ." [16]

The first two basic questions which philosophy attempts to answer are: Where did I come from; who am I? If we arrived by chance and exist for nothing, then why are we here? What is the purpose of our existence, our reason for being, our motivation for living? This is something each of us must know!

WHY AM I HERE?

One man whose ideas have shaped the destiny of nations was a German who died almost a hundred years ago and whose funeral was attended by only six or seven people. Karl Marx, Hegel's prize pupil, believed we are here to produce social changes by class struggles. He viewed the world and man's place in it as a continuous involvement in overthrowing capitalism. He believed that the evils of society all flow from private ownership of property and consequently our individual lives should be devoted to abolishing free enterprise.

The theories which Marx put into action resulted in some of the most inhumane actions of man toward man known in the history of the world. The results have exploded into global conflict of man against man and nation against nation.

Marx knew why he was here. When he was asked by someone what his objective in life was he said, "To dethrone God and destroy capitalism." [17]

What kind of a world are we in that has more than half of its population fervently believing that Marx is the answer? I believe this is a major reason we have moved into the "Terminal Generation."

The philosophical battleground of the century has been established in the Hegelian method (conflict will produce change), Darwinian nature (an impersonal beginning), the Marxian society (destroy free enterprise) and the unknowable God of Kierkegaard. The frontal attack is then possible for Sigmund Freud who explained that the mind is as much of a battleground as external forces.

Freud saw our repressed feelings struggling for existence in the unconscious—a superego which is unable to contain these feelings —and this results in lives of ever-increasing guilt. In other words, if we suppress what we really feel we will live under the burden of guilt.

There is no doubt that the intellects of these leading proponents of modern thought were sharp and incisive. However, their mood was one of despair; one college textbook in the humanities calls our era the Age of Anxiety.

The thinkers and philosophers themselves became the products of their own teachings. Kierkegaard said, "I want to go into a madhouse to see if the profundity of madness will not disclose the solution to life's riddle." [18]

He also offered his own definition of purpose, his personal answer to "Why am I here?" Soren Kierkegaard, the Protestant theologian who introduced existentialism to both secular and religious thought, said, "The purpose of life is to be brought to the highest degree of disgust with life." [19]

If this is the conclusion, then everything is chaotic, purposeless, and absurd. Check it out. This is the world view of many people today. Listen to the classroom lectures—discern these views from some modern pulpits—read the philosophies in textbooks and best-sellers.

With this prelude of ideas, how is man able to answer the last great question of life?

WHERE AM I GOING?

Friedrich Nietzsche (1844–1900) was another German who fostered some explosive ideas. He prepared his country for the rise of Hitler and made the shattering pronouncement, "God is dead." He glorified a superman and his power, which provided the basic philosophy upon which Hitler built his slogan: WE ARE THE MASTER RACE.

The terror of the Third Reich demonstrated that the philosophies of one generation can become the motivating force directing the activists in another generation.

Where did Nietzsche see man's direction? He said, "Our whole culture has been moving for some time now, with a tortured tension that is growing from decade to decade, as toward a catastrophe: restlessly, violently, headlong, like a river that wants to reach the end, that no longer reflects, that is afraid to reflect." [20]

Step by step we see the very men who contributed to the growth of despair and the Age of Anxiety agonizing over the results of their own philosophies. It's like a parent who has never provided guidelines, discipline, or direction for his child, suddenly waking up one day to discover the unhappy human being he has helped mold.

Kierkegaard himself despaired: "One might say perhaps that there lives not one single man who after all is not to some extent in despair, in whose inmost parts there does not dwell a disquietude, a discord, an anxious dread of an unknown something." [21]

The despair of Kierkegaard was even more agonizing than some of the others, for he was a theologian. What a shame that he evidently didn't believe the Scriptures which say:

> Be anxious for nothing, but in everything by prayer and supplication with thanksgiving let your requests be made known to God. And the peace of God, which surpasses all comprehension, shall guard your hearts and your minds in Christ Jesus.
>
>   Philippians 4:6, 7

Darwin said we evolved from lower species and that nature is in a struggle for existence; Marx said that society is in a constant class struggle; Nietzsche proclaimed that God is dead and that "one must die several times while still alive." [22] Kierkegaard found life disgusting.

Whether we realize it or not, these are among the philosophies which have become the basis for the world view of modern education. This view permeates through our school systems in every academic discipline. As it does, it produces the same uncertainty, the same confusion of mind which it did in those men who formulated the philosophies.

In everything which touches our lives we are reaping the harvest from the seeds these men and their disciples have sown. The alarming thing is that most people don't understand or realize this.

Jim, home from the university with his new thoughts, has discarded any absolute values. Linda, searching for her own identity, has gravitated toward a cult. Pat, without knowing her own self-worth, has abandoned her role as a wife and mother to follow some path to despair.

No wonder historian Arnold Toynbee said, "Our present form of society is truly repulsive . . . the formidable fundamental question now is: 'What is life for?' " [23]

No wonder there is so little acceptance of God and His absolutes within the confines of our secondary and higher education.

No wonder so few persons today—no matter what their background may be—are able to answer in a positive and healthy way the four great questions of life:

Where did I come from?
Who am I?
Why am I here?
Where am I going?

How about you? Can you answer those questions? If you struggle with them yourself, don't give up. There are answers, and by the time you've finished this book I hope you'll know them.

The certain answers to these four great questions are vital for a positive mental attitude. The physical well-being and the spiritual direction of everyone who discovers those answers will be enhanced. With that discovery, anxiety will turn to peace and despair will be replaced by hope.

Hope is what gives life motivation, purpose, and enthusiasm—and that's what this book is all about!

The world is a looking glass, and gives back to every man the reflection of his own face . . . .

WILLIAM THACKERAY

3

We Are the Way We Are

Communication is so important that lives are shattered by lack of it—men succeed or fail according to their ability to use it. Communication contains the greatest power for good and the strongest agent for evil.

Several years ago I became interested in the practical fallout of philosophical thought bombs. Since writing briefly about this in *Satan Is Alive and Well on Planet Earth* I have been more attuned to the results in our contemporary life.

As we look at the impact of so much nineteenth- and twentieth-century philosophy on every aspect of today's world, you may be asking, "What difference does it make to me?" Maybe you have a solid faith in God and believe that certain pursuits are for others, but not for you. Perhaps you would rather just tune out what is unpleasant—avoid any negatives.

How can we communicate if we don't understand where a person's at? If you have children, think about them. They are surrounded with these thought forms in their classrooms, on television, in the movies, from music, magazines, and friends. How can any of us establish understanding if we remain blinded to the bombardment of ideas surrounding them?

You owe it to your children to understand what they are being exposed to.

PREDICTABLE RESULTS

If we leave a piece of iron outside, exposed to the rain and wind, it will rust. If we release a light bulb from our hand, it will fall. If we don't eat, we'll starve. The laws of chemistry and physics produce definite results.

In the same way, the impact of such men as Kant, Hegel, Kierkegaard, Darwin, Marx, Dewey, Freud, Camus, Sartre, Russell, Nietzsche, and others can clearly be seen in our Age of Anxiety.

33

Here's the equation: anxiety minus an answer equals despair. Look at a worried parent, for instance. His child started a pattern of rebellion which led him into the drug scene. The cycle began with drugs to booze . . . detention hall to jail . . . out on parole . . . back on drugs . . . then disappearance. Weeks of searching have led to no solution. Under the circumstances, a deep inner despair engulfs the mother and father.

With anyone who is seeking for solutions to the everyday complications of living in a complex world, the end result is the same.

In many cases despair is the predecessor of violence—inner turmoil or outward effects. And that's where so many are today, programmed into despair, pointed in the direction of violence.

It's no wonder we are the way we are.

The fact that has amazed me is that many of the prominent idea communicators today recognize this despair themselves. I do not consider myself a critic or a judge, but an observer of the current scene. The communicators themselves are their own critics.

DESPAIR IN ART

I was talking to a friend of mine, a businessman, who had recently returned from a trip to Holland. His wife had dragged him through some art museums and for the first time in his life he began to develop an interest in the Great Masters. He went to the Ryksmuseum in Amsterdam and told me how he stood with awe looking at Rembrandt's famous *Night Watch*.

Shortly after my friend's trip someone wielded a knife on that great painting, slashing the figures in a bizarre attempt to deface their beauty.

Modern artists, however, do not desecrate with a knife; they exhibit despair and violence in their own creations. Francis Bacon, the modern artist who has been acclaimed as a "new idol" of the New York art world, said, "I've always wanted and never succeeded in painting the smile." [24]

Bacon, who by his own admission is a compulsive gambler, a hard drinker and homosexual, says that "One's basic nature is totally without hope . . . ." He exemplifies this mood in his paintings, which prompted an art critic to comment that ". . . in your work . . . most people seem to feel there's somehow a distinct presence or threat of violence."

Bacon replied, ". . . I have been accustomed to always living through forms of violence—which may or may not have an effect upon one, but I think probably does . . . ."

When he was asked the pointed question of what his painting is all about he answers, "It's concerned with my kind of psyche, it's concerned with my kind of—I'm putting it in a very pleasant way—exhilarated despair." [25]

Andy Warhol, modern artist, has been called the *Nothingness Himself*. He is described as a mirror and *Newsweek* magazine says:

> . . . What he does see is the image of himself that has been created by his critics, both those who admire him as a shrewd and perversely subtle image maker, and those who despise him as a shrewd and satanically subtle manipulator of a corrupted culture that can no longer distinguish between excellence, and trash.[26]

> When you look at Warhol's art you see how much has indeed been erased from both art and reality in modern times. Rembrandt looked at a human face and used the most exquisite skills to body forth its meaning and his compassion. Warhol looks—not at the face itself, but at the innumerable images of that face . . . he has created chic icons for empty people to decorate their emptiness . . . .[27]

Warhol's reputation and his art are based on shock value. At a time when every trade, every business must have a "philosophy," Andy is the superstar of *chic freakiness*. At his best he is said to capture the pathos, the garish beauty, and something of the terror of society.

A few years ago I had an explosive encounter with a UCLA student of modern art. I was speaking at the free speech platform there on the campus when suddenly he came running out of the crowd toward me shouting threats and obscenities. Some of my friends had to grab him and hold him down. He was furious!

He had read what I had written in *Satan Is Alive and Well on Planet Earth* about modern art and was violently angry about some of my statements.

About a year after this incident the same art student came up to me after a talk and said, "Do you remember me?" I didn't, but then he told me about the time he had tried to attack me at the free speech platform. I immediately remembered the incident. He was completely changed, however, and apologized for his violent behavior. "I know what you mean, now," he said. "My view of God and His world has changed—and so has my personal understanding of art."

Art shows a man's view of reality; it is a mirror of the generation. Most of modern art according to many artists themselves reflects the trend of despair.

Art is the reflection of why *we are the way we are.*

DESPAIR IN MUSIC

Of all the art forms music has given in to anxiety with great abandon. Modern music broke with old techniques and established new ones; it is characterized by the frequent use of dissonance, leaving the listener with a feeling of aimlessness.

Corrie ten Boom, the world-renowned Dutch author, told me that during times of personal despair she would sit down at her piano and play Bach. The music was soothing and soon she would feel a deep contentment.

Today we find that much of what we hear on popular radio stations and in the record shops is music without melody, or rhythm without music. The lyrics in particular reveal the aimlessness; they are mostly repetitions of one phrase or sentence which are designed to arouse the animal passions.

Sex rock is the big thing. *Time* magazine said, "Just a twist of the AM dial demonstrates how far things have gone. On the average 15 percent of air time is devoted to songs like 'Do It Any Way You Wanna,' 'Let's Do It Again,' 'That's the Way I like It,' and 'I Want'a Do Something Freaky to You.'"

What kind of reactions can we expect from our teenagers when the once-innocent radio now vibrates with what is aptly described as "orgasmic rock"? [28]

Another music phenomenon of recent times is that of the drug-inspired occultic music. One group, called the Eagles, is the product of the newest intellectual fashion spawned from the writings of a young intellectual, Carlos Castaneda, whose master's thesis at the University of California became one of the best-selling books of the early seventies.

How could music be the end result of the work of an anthropologist, Castaneda? As in all art forms, music is both the result and the cause of the philosophy of its age. "The Eagles were conceived in the teachings of Carlos Castaneda and his ephemeral medicine man Don Juan." [29]

The five young musicians, all in their twenties, spent long, sleepless nights in the desert, indulging in raw tequila and peyote, studying the sorcery of Don Juan, the mysterious old Yaqui Indian who supposedly taught Castaneda. Out of the influence of the occult and the drug inspiration have come the songs and music which have resulted in the Eagles becoming a top U.S. rock band.

The philosophy of their music, which reaches into the ears and lives of millions of teens and preteens, is that of "loneliness, excess, and self-destruction." [30]

Why is rock music so important in determining the results of the directional thinking of the past generation? Because it, above all other types of music, represents the point where the thinking of many of our young people is centered.

Another new rock star, Bruce Springsteen, is described by a national magazine in this way: ". . . His music is primal, directly in touch with all the impulses of wild humor and glancing melancholy, street tragedy and punk anarchy that have made rock the distinctive voice of a generation." [31]

Springsteen once cautioned in a song that you can "waste your summer prayin' in vain for a savior to rise from these streets."

That's it—the universal voice of need—the need for purpose— for a reason for existence—for a "savior to rise from these streets."

In the university classrooms the students may be immersed in their studies of the arts and humanities, trying to unravel the complexities of thought expressed in these fields, without realizing that the thought which has resulted in their rock heroes has also affected classical forms.

Music, for instance, in the more classical sense, has emerged from the Dadaism of the twentieth century, just as art has done. *Dada,* a randomly chosen word, actually has a nonsense meaning as related to art. Dadaism is an art form composed without design, senseless, and capable of producing disgust in whatever one of our senses it reaches, whether the eye or the ear.

Students of the humanities are introduced to *Neo-Dadaism,* which means a new or updated form of this art of the "nothingness" in music, through the nonconformist content of a composer such as John Cage.

Cage typifies Neo-Dadaism in music with compositions where an electric wire coil and twelve radios dialed to different frequencies are used in the performances. His "Variations IV" includes "fragments of Schubert, traffic noises, jazz, telephone bells, Christmas carols, static, a receding train, screams, and the Blue Danube Waltz." [32]

Cage is to music what Andy Warhol is to pop art. It is the Art of the Nothingness. These art forms reflect the search, the emptiness, the distinctive voice of a generation.

Music is the voice of *the way we are.*

DESPAIR AND DISASTER IN THE CINEMA

The reviews the film industry gives in its own professional journals play a recurring theme. Frustration, despair, a meaningless existence are thrown on the screen in a kaleidoscope of blurred colors. The movies aren't what they used to be, but they are what we should expect them to be. Reflections. Imitations of life.

The melody played in the themes of the cinema is a dissonant sound, just as Warhol and the Eagles exhibit their cries on art and music. In a recent film, *Fake,* shown at the famous Cannes Film Festival, a review stated that if this film, which is questioned as being "a fake Orson Welles" is truly a fake and not produced by Welles at all, then the film suggests that nothing is true. The entire premise of this film, which was a hit in Paris cinemas, was that there is nothing—no one who can be believed.

With nothing being true, the hopelessness of existence is the progressive result. Michelangelo Antonioni, a famous director of some important message films, has a pervading philosophy which begins with his characters' feeling the distress of simply being human, ". . . unable to experience the world as anything but habitually apart from one's self," and then going into a hopeless state. There is no lasting relief from the despair which is present in every life.[33]

In the art of animation films, there is a repetition of the same message. First prize in the world-wide animation festival went to a film called *The Footprint* by Jacques Cardon. It is a comment on oppression which is simple but very effective. A covering is removed from the back of the head of a young boy revealing a deep footprint from the boot of his oppressor, who makes the boy kneel in order to press his heavy shoe on his head.

This isn't exactly Disney fare, but it won the prize!

A Hollywood director whose work bears his individual philosophic stamp is Sidney Pollack. In an article ironically titled "The Way We Are" in *Film Comment*, the statement is made, "As a group, Pollack's films are informed by a pervasive skepticism concerning man's ability to discover a meaningful existence." [33a]

Pollack is a commentator on the American experience, his concern has been with man's search for values in a disintegrating world. One of his most pessimistic works was *They Shoot Horses, Don't They?* During a comparatively short time in the Hollywood big time, Pollack has made significant contributions to the philosophical thought of man's fate in an impersonal world in such films as *This Property Is Condemned, Jeremiah Johnson,* and *Three Days of the Condor.*

A generation of despair. In a review of a Western movie, the lead characters are said to embody "the random life-style of this undirected generation." This new-style Western has no relation to the "white hats and the black hats" of the past generation—the flick where the heroine is threatened with losing her ranch, the rustlers are the bad guys, and the hero rides a Palomino. Today the outlaws are a couple of "middle-class types in Stetsons" and their families. ". . . their elders, affluent and inert, have realized the American Dream and don't know what to do next, so like aimlessly fired bullets, they go ricocheting about a West where even the dream is gone." [34]

From despair to violence. We have the wave of disaster films now: *Towering Inferno, Jaws, Poseidon Adventure, Earthquake.* And when they run out we will have them all over again in an even more shocking sequel, just as we had *Godfather* and *Godfather 2.*

Movies have done everything, shown everything, and have left nothing unsaid or undone. A review of one movie in *Time* magazine reveals that sheer insanity has invaded the cinema arts. Of this movie it is said, it is ". . . full of unenlightened lunacy, is not really a film at all. It is a social disease." [35]

Movies are an imitation of the way we are.

DESPAIR AND DISTRESS IN THE PRESS

A good friend of mine, a graduate from a prestigious journalism school in the late forties told me they were taught that there was a difference between straight news stories and editorials. One was fact, the other was opinion. This was so basic that any reflection of personal opinion creeping into a news report was immediately given a failing grade.

Today our newspapers express opinions in the straight reporting of events. Distrust of factual reporting is so widespread that most people can't believe what they read.

The press has also gone to extremes in what is printed. Pornography is big business, but the promoters of every known vice are continually coming up with new shockers for our hardened generation. A young editor of a new magazine advocates drug usage, describes the effects of various drugs, and even advertises where to get them. In easy disregard for the truth, he is quoted as saying, ". . . we do not lead our readers into drugs." [36] However, I obtained a copy of this publication at a campus bookstore and was amazed that such damaging information was contained in a magazine easily obtainable by any young person.

The thrust of a publication like this exponent of the drug culture is toward readers who "enjoy getting high and having a good time," according to the editor. He says that future issues will cover articles on voodoo drugs, erotic art in the Vatican, and getting high on death. The latter statement alone is enough to arouse serious concern.[36a]

The state of the publications industry, driven by economic pressures and reflecting the trend in society, has resulted in some large printers' taking on nudity magazines as clients. In the case of one company which had previously printed home and farming magazines, some employees asked not to be assigned to jobs involving the nude-filled magazines. These employees based their action on their personal religious and moral convictions and were consequently fired for their stand. One of the fired employees said, "I'm unhappy with what they (the company) have done . . . They've been a family magazine company for quite a few years and now they're tearing down everything they built up . . . . They're definitely aiding in corrupting people's minds." [37]

A generation ago the *True Romance* and *True Confession* magazines were under-the-bed reading for thousands. The mildly suggestive stories in these racy publications of the thirties and forties have been transported into the respectable slicks of the seventies. There is little restraint in language; descriptive stories of every degree of moral deprivation are common in the media.

The press is an echo of why *we are the way we are.*

WHAT ABOUT EDUCATION?

Modern education is the pulpit from which many teachers and professors have evangelized students to the relative thinking of the nineteenth-century philosophers.

Education today is designed to produce changed beliefs. The teaching method is the conflict/change theory, which is right out of the Hegelian philosophy of thesis-antithesis-synthesis. The idea in the classrooms is to present conflicting opinions on race, religion, morals, law, history, and allow the student to come to his own conclusion.

In the state of California a study was recently made on the classroom results of existentialist ideas. Here's what happens: the student is taught that on the basis of conflicting opinions, he is to make a free choice of what to believe. He is to be free from the ideas and beliefs of his parents, church and society's norms. He is taught the so-called truth-searching process where he will consult the group's opinions, he will gather knowledge scientifically, and make a decision based upon this information and his own personal preferences.

Law, lessons of history, and biblical truths are completely omitted as valid in arriving at a decision.

"It's all in the way you look at it." "That's just your opinion." These are common phrases which deny absolutes by implication.

The conflict/change method is being used in almost every subject being taught in the schools.

In history, for instance, the past is not used as a source of precise data, but as information from which the student creates the past by his own view of historical events. The young person is given information about conflicting life-styles, beliefs, and governments, none of which are good or evil, except in his view.

What about reading courses? The primary aim is to introduce materials which will arouse a child's own way of looking at things.

A book recommended in teacher-training to teach "values" gives us the exact trend being fostered in our schools. "The point has been made that our values tend to be a product of our experiences. They are not just a matter of true or false." Also: "The person is pushed to examine the history of his beliefs or attitudes, to look at their origins, and to see if they are really his or if they might have been absorbed unthinkingly." [38]

In other words, our children are being taught that *values* (which in itself is an abstract notion or idea, not a solid *principle*) are neither right nor wrong, and that beliefs (particularly if they are taught at home or church) must be reexamined.

Even our grade-school children are being prepared in this philosophy. A "very different and interesting teaching approach" used in the Los Angeles city school system to "encourage creative expression" said of the child, ". . . His answer is always accepted since there is no right or wrong answer." [38a]

In our schools and universities, brilliant men who are thoroughly committed to a world view without God, highly skilled in their teaching methods, are convincing to their young, impressionable students.

With Jesus Christ only mentioned in the classroom as swear words, with the Bible barred or ridiculed, it's no wonder that the pervading influence of our schools is devastating to the majority of our youth.

Stripped of absolutes, left to choice, questioning values and omitting principles, it's no wonder we have appalling outbreaks of violence at most schools. No wonder they have become spawning grounds for drugs. No wonder it's almost impossible to keep discipline and order on the campuses. Students are adrift in a sea of moral confusion.

I observed firsthand the bizarre phenomena of the results of many professors' teaching in the university classrooms an anti-God, humanistic form of Marxism which implied a violent overthrow of the society. I watched with grim fascination when the student activists started putting into action the philosophies they had been taught. They rioted, blew up buildings, and burned down banks. When the very professors who had fed these students the ideas expressed concern, the students rightly called them *hypocrites*.

Fortune magazine described in careful terms the way most people view our modern educational system. It said that our current malaise is "that peculiar mixture of cynicism, fatigue, and sadness with which we now view education." [39]

It's the educational system that first injected these destructive philosophies of Marx, Darwin, Kant, Hegel, and so forth, into our society.

It continues to fashion men who may have great artistic, musical, acting, journalistic, or legislative talents into relative thinkers without definite moral principles.

More than any other vehicle of our society, I believe that the educational system is most guilty of spreading the modern way of thinking today.

After all, where did the Bacons, Warhols, Eagles, Castanedas, and so forth, first get their philosophical base for their world view? It was through the schools, particularly their colleges.

Our educational system is an indication of why we are what we are.

Art is the reflection . . .
Music is the voice . . .
The movies are the imitation . . .
The press is the echo . . .
Education is the indication . . .
. . . of why we are the way we are.

INSIDE VIEW

There's no denying it, our society is deteriorating rapidly. What we have examined in this chapter doesn't begin to cover all the moral and social ills of our day. Truly the disease is terminal for this generation.

Most of the sources which have described the present situation in this chapter are the way secular communicators see themselves. If this were all that we had to follow the future would be bleak—utterly hopeless. However, there is *hope*—solid, strengthening, certain hope.

You have probably guessed by now that we were going to talk about the hope found in the Bible. You may have been wondering about the crescendo of despair and have been tempted to clamp your hands over your ears and shut your eyes. I wouldn't blame you. However, if we are to recognize the validity of the hope which is present and also the hope which is coming, we need to see how the present world condition is fitting into the predicted biblical pattern.

The Bible tells us of many events, many trends, and specific happenings which will precede a time when Jesus the Messiah will return and bring in a whole new world order. This new world will not be devised by politicians or maneuvered by men. This world will be one where despair and violence will be erased.

However, one of the predictions of the age preceding the great event which we know as the Second Coming of Christ, is the disintegration of our society.

In this passage the Apostle Paul predicted the moral decay of our world. In this prophecy we see the impact of man's choice to push God and His Word out of his life and memory.

> But mark this: There will be terrible times in the last days. People will be lovers of themselves, lovers of money, boastful, proud, abusive, disobedient to their parents, ungrateful, unholy, without love, unforgiving, slanderous, without self-control, brutal, not lovers of the good, treacherous, rash, conceited, lovers of pleasure rather than lovers of God—having a form of godliness but denying its power. Have nothing to do with them.
>
> 2 Timothy 3:1–5 NIV

What happens when a society rejects God? It's either truth or the consequences—only this is reality, not a game. Paul lists the consequences:

> Furthermore, since they did not think it worthwhile to retain the knowledge of God, he gave them over to a depraved mind, to do what ought not to be done. They have become filled with every kind of wickedness, evil, greed and depravity. They are full of envy, murder, strife, deceit and malice. They are gossips, slanderers, God-haters, insolent, arrogant and boastful; they invent ways of doing evil; they disobey their parents; they are senseless, faithless, heartless, ruthless. Although they know God's righteous decree that those who do such things deserve death, they not only continue to do these very things, but also approve of those who practice them.
>
> Romans 1:28–32 NIV

Those are rough consequences! Thank God that in spite of the growing darkness, there is a light at the end of the tunnel. There *is* hope for the Terminal Generation. God knows what's happening—He predicted it. God also has a plan to right all wrong and deliver everyone who trusts in Him.

And you may be a part of His plan—the choice is up to you. Things may be grim now, but the Psalmist said long ago:

> . . . Weeping may last for the night,
> But a shout of joy comes in the morning.
> Psalms 30:5

The cynic says, "Joy? Don't hand me that pie-in-the-sky stuff." The optimist says, "It's all the way you look at things—the world is getting better."

But the person who knows Jesus Christ as his Lord can be a realist and still shout for joy! He can also be ready for whatever happens. The Bible urges:

> Therefore, prepare your minds for action; be self-controlled; set your hope fully on the grace to be given you when Jesus Christ is revealed.
>
> 1 Peter 1:13 NIV

These two crises—the political and the spiritual—are occurring simultaneously. It is our generation that will have to confront them.

ALEKSANDR SOLZHENITSYN,
exiled Russian author, in
Reader's Digest, December, 1975

. . . "Tell us," they said, "when will this happen, and what will be the sign of your coming and of the end of the age?"

Matthew 24:3 NIV
His Disciples questioning Jesus

4

Copeless

At the very time when our minds have been programmed for despair, when our intellects have been bombarded by moral depravity, when we are least able to cope with the stress of our lives, the greatest crises in history are coming upon us! When universal chaos is the most threatening, mentally and intellectually we are least able to meet and handle the threat.

Worldwide unrest grows with each passing hour. This generation is moving toward persistent pessimism.

However, before anyone becomes buried in oppressive gloom, let me reemphasize that there is genuine ground for hope, optimism, and a whole new excitement about life *right now*. All of these present and coming crises were predicted long ago. We can have complete assurance and peace of mind *if* we are properly related to God. He has told us where all of this is going to end and given us a positive knowledge of what to expect.

It's vitally important to all of us, as I will show later, to know how we can be delivered from the worst part of the coming world catastrophes.

It's exciting to be alive now and watch events unfold which were predicted over a period of thirty-five hundred to two thousand years ago. How full of hope it makes me to see history conforming into a precisely foretold plan and to know that nothing is going to happen by blind purposeless chance.

Many times I have been asked, "If you could rewrite *The Late Great Planet Earth* and *There's a New World Coming* today would you change any of the prophetic views?"

The manuscript for *The Late Great Planet Earth* was finished on November 1, 1969. The prophetic patterns and the future trends depicted in this book become clearer as history unfolds. This is also true of *There's a New World Coming*. I wouldn't change a thing.

Here are some of the signs which the Bible says will occur in the period preceding the visible return of Jesus Christ to this earth.

International realignment of nations into four spheres of political power—which would occur in the same general era as the rebirth of the state of Israel.

Israel would have an incredible enemy to its "uttermost north" which would gather around it a number of allies. (This is Russia.)

The Arabs and the Black African nations (King of the South) would be the avowed enemies of the revived State of Israel.

At the same time biblical prophecy refers to another sphere of power which will arise, the Kings of the East, or China and the Oriental forces.

As all these spheres of power become prominent there will be a ten-nation confederacy formed out of the countries which comprised the Roman Empire. I believe this could be the European Common Market.

(At the present there are nine Common Market countries. However, a small article in the February 10, 1976, issue of the Wall Street Journal takes on great significance. It said, "Greece's bid to join the Common Market was endorsed by all nine members." It continues to say that negotiations on membership terms will probably take at least a year. And that would make ten nations in the Common Market!)

There will be widespread crime and moral depravations.

There will be famines and earthquakes in increasing frequency.

There will be an increase in the occult, false religions, and the supernatural.

These are all a part of the prophecy pattern.

The events which are accelerating in the latter half of the 1970s are fitting perfectly into the pattern predicted by the ancient

Hebrew prophets of the Bible. They indicate that this is certainly the general time of unprecedented worldwide catastrophes which are to usher in the coming of the Messiah and His Kingdom.

A RIDDLE SOLVED

One of the most unexplainable elements which I encountered in the beginning of the study of prophecy was that the whole pattern of the future world events centered its emphasis around the Middle East.

The reborn State of Israel was central to the development of world events which are predicted to lead to the last and greatest war of all time.

How could the rather backward and undeveloped Arab countries, together with the small State of Israel, become the dominant interest of the great industrial powers of the world? It was puzzling to me. I thought to myself, who wants all that useless sand? Even with the oil, the countries seemed incapable of drawing the Western powers into that arena in any significant manner.

However, this very concentration of influence and power is in biblical prophecy.

In 1973 what should have been obvious became clear. The way the Middle East would initially become a dominant world power was through its vast oil reserves.

The Achilles' heel of the great industrial nations of the West is oil. We literally have based our whole economy on oil; everything from energy to synthetic clothing to farm fertilizers is dependent upon this commodity. It is the lifeblood of the developed world.

When the Arabs formed the first successful cartel and shut off the oil supply, the great powers panicked. Western European nations and Japan immediately began to try and make terms with the various Arab oil nations. Then the Arabs, along with Iran, brought the free-world powers to their knees by increasing the price of oil fourfold. This almost destroyed the economies of Western Europe and Japan and sent the USA into a very serious recession-inflation syndrome.

ECONOMIC HAVOC

1974 and 1975 witnessed the most rapid transferral of capital in history. The Middle East oil-producing nations raked in billions of dollars from Western Europe, Japan, and the USA. This was a great deal more money than they could actually use. Potentially the greatest danger posed by the Organization of Petroleum Exporting Countries (OPEC) led by the Arabs is the unprecedented accumulation of excess money.

To give some idea of this potential threat, Ernest Conine wrote in the October 25, 1974, *Los Angeles Times,*

> As recently as 1973, countries of the Arab-led oil cartel had only a 4 billion-dollar surplus available for investment outside their own borders. This year the figure will jump to $55 billion; by the end of 1976 it is expected to reach $200 billion. Within 10 years according to a confidential study by the World Bank, this handful of small countries could have more than $1 trillion on hand—more than enough to buy all the shares outstanding on the New York Stock Exchange.
>
> From "Will the Arabs Buy the U.S.?"

No wonder Henry Ford II said, "Arabs may end up in control of most of the big companies of this country." [40] The Arabs have tried already to purchase controlling interest in the Lockheed Corporation, which is the largest military hardware contractor in America.[40a] What this would mean in times of a national emergency, particularly involving Israel, is clear to see.

The same sort of financial invasion is taking shape in Western Europe. Iran recently purchased a 25 percent interest in Krupp steel works, one of the biggest industrial enterprises in West Germany.[40b] It is also a militarily strategic factor.

A SELF-FEEDING DISASTER

The clear and apparent danger, especially for Western Europe and Japan, is the enormous outflow of capital to Arab countries to sustain their vast oil needs. The trade deficit created by this has almost bankrupt Italy, and put most of the other Western countries into serious economic trouble.

The cycle runs like this: the more the price of oil is increased and money flows into the OPEC countries, the more in debt other nations will become. As the trade deficit builds up, money must be borrowed. The only significantly large amounts of money available for loans on the international scene is from OPEC members. The more borrowed from OPEC members, the more a country is forced to bend to OPEC's will. Eventually they could force great industrial countries to pay off by allowing purchases of major corporations.

The Arabs have two trump aces. They can gradually bend the industrial nations to their will by the enormous accumulation of petrodollars while building up great trade deficits in them. The second ace is that they can instantly strangle the nations at will by shutting off the oil supply, watching from the sidelines while the nations cut each other's throats by seeking special deals.

What is the significance? The Arabs and their Moslem brother, Iran, can trouble the world with whatever troubles them. The number-one item which continually irritates them is the State of Israel, with the Jewish possession of Old Jerusalem the most painful thorn.

At every meeting of the OPEC nations the question of how to use "the oil weapon" against Israel has been a major item for discussion. An obvious indication of intent is that large sums of money have been contributed to the so-called confrontation countries (Egypt, Syria, Jordan, and Lebanon) to purchase the latest military equipment. The liberation of Palestine has been and will remain a matter of sacred Moslem honor to the Arabs.

ISRAEL'S GROWING PERIL

With the enormous growth of Arab power through oil and money, the position of Israel has become more desperate than at any time since her rebirth as a nation. Using their great strategic weapon of oil blackmail, the Arabs have managed to turn almost all nations against Israel. At least they have neutralized most who would have offered aid previously.

Even verbal condemnation of Israel has been forced. This became obvious when Japan, after the Yom Kippur War of October 1973, slapped Israel with strong censure.

One of the most obvious ways of illustrating the changed world picture since the Arab oil embargo of 1973–74 is the refusal of any European nation to allow U.S. C5s to land and refuel. The only thing that saved Israel from disaster in the Yom Kippur War was the amazing resupply effort of the U.S. using the giant C5-cargo planes. These planes had to refuel once in each trip from the U.S. because of the huge cargo load they were carrying. Every European country refused to allow these planes to land and refuel except Portugal, who allowed them to land in the Azores Island base; the other countries were too afraid to lose Arab oil.

Now look at the picture: the government of Portugal has changed and the new regime is not favorable to Israel or the USA. In the event of a new war there could be a disaster, or a major change in U.S. involvement. We might have to commit the U.S. Sixth Fleet with its marines and aircraft to stop an Arab overrun of Israel. If the USA becomes involved, the Russians will seize the opportunity to move into the Middle East with an avalanche of military power. (This would be an indication that Armageddon is close.)

The people of Israel sense their growing isolation; they feel friendless in an ocean of hostile Arabs. Only the USA remains as a friend to be counted in time of need. However, there are alarming sounds from some quarters of the U.S. Some powerful forces in this country are seriously questioning why supporting Israel is in our strategic interests.

In the United States there are only two major forces which are pushing for the support of Israel: one is the Jewish population and the other is the evangelical believer in Jesus Christ who believes that it is prophetic necessity for Israel to be established as a state in their ancient homeland.

An interesting statement with accurate insight was made by Meir Kahane, the founder of the Jewish Defense League:

Israel has within the United States a weapon that itself believes in and can convince others that the U.S.'s true interest is total and unconditional backing for the Jewish State. It is a weapon that disdains talk of oil and real politik and eschews these for the real interest—the Christian one.

I refer to the tens of fundamentalist and evangelical Christian sects, whose members number in the millions and whose leaders have national and international prestige and influence (Billy Graham is merely the most obvious example.) These are groups who are totally Bible-oriented, who believe that the Bible is the literal Word of God and to whom the biblical prophecies of a return to Zion by the Jewish people and the setting up a Jewish State are absolute preconditions for the final redemption.[41]

Whether these two forces are enough to sway public opinion over to an armed intervention in the Middle East in the event of an overrun or invasion of Israel is at best tenuous.

THE SAMSON COMPLEX

As Israel looks at her deteriorating position, a new mentality seems to be emerging. For years the news media has labelled the Israeli attitude of defense as a *Masada Complex*. This refers to the fortress which was the last bastion of Israel's resistance to Rome. When it fell in A.D. 73 the defenders all took their own lives rather than surrender to slavery under Rome. It reflects the fight-to-the-death determination.

This is no longer Israel's mood. While on a recent trip to Israel I had the opportunity to talk with one of their most courageous and brilliant generals. He told me about Israel's new attitude which he called the *Samson Complex*. When Samson died he destroyed all his enemies with himself.

If that characteristic were translated into the perilous powder keg of the current Middle East situation, imagine what would happen. It is easy to see why Israel would feel a Samson Complex. The Israelis see the world turning against them; they are completely surrounded and outnumbered by a race which has been hostile toward them for the better part of four thousand years. The Arabs have almost unlimited financial backing for military equipment which they can purchase from numerous sources. The Arabs can turn nations against them by their oil power.

On the other hand, Israel is entirely dependent upon the USA for military supplies and the U.S. has been reluctant to sell them anything more than a twenty-day supply. Israel feels that if the Arabs break through their defenses that the world will stand by while they are massacred.

Not only does Israel feel that in a final showdown the USA would desert her, but the Arabs believe this, too. This is reflected in an article entitled, "An Israeli View of Vietnam's Lesson." It says: "Syrian president Hafez Al-Assad made no secret of his attitude. He represents the Arab school of thought that views the U.S. impotence in the ultimate phase of the Vietnam tragedy as proof that in the last resort America would abandon Israel, just as it abandoned Cambodia and Vietnam." [42]

THE WORLD'S WORST-KEPT SECRET

With these facts staring them in the face, many experts believe that Israel has assembled a considerable nuclear arsenal with which she will, in the light of an imminent defeat, destroy everything around her as Samson did the Philistines.

A scientist from California Institute of Technology recently told me that many believe Israel has the neutron bomb, which in terms of destroying human beings is the ultimate weapon. It can absolutely demolish all protein-bearing living things in a predetermined area from one to 100 square miles without destroying buildings and terrain. It also would be preferred over nuclear and thermonuclear weapons because it does not leave the contamination of radio activity.

In terms of the prophetic pattern, Israel is rapidly fitting into its final role. Zechariah predicted that all nations would be drawn into the final great war which begins with a dispute between the Arabs and Israel over Jerusalem. (See Zechariah 12:2, 3.)

The Prophet Joel also speaks of all nations being drawn into war over Israel and their armies being destroyed there. (See Joel 3:1–17.) This is a major theme of prophecy in several Bible passages.

THE FALSE HOPE OF ISRAEL

According to prophecy, the reborn state of Israel will be forced by ever-increasing peril to sign a defense treaty with the coming dictator of the revived Roman Empire, composed of a ten-nation confederacy, which Bible scholars believe is developing through the European Common Market now. This will prove to be a curse from which only the returning Messiah can deliver them.

THE THIRD-WORLD THREAT

A very significant factor which has rapidly materialized recently is the increasing prominence of many Third World nations, particularly African, who have thrown their backing with the Arabs against Israel.

As we described in *The Late Great Planet Earth*, the prophets Ezekiel and Daniel both predicted a confederacy of the Arabs and many black African countries into a sphere of power which would seek to destroy Israel. In fact, the first stage of the world's last holocaust is to be initiated by this power bloc, called "the king of the South," according to Daniel 11:40–45.

Since the preceding interpretation was noted in 1969, significant developments have occurred to fulfill this prophetic trend. For one thing, Russia has become the number-one arms supplier to the Third World. "Twenty years after its entry into the Middle East arms market, the Soviet Union has steadily boosted sales to become the No. 1 supplier of weapons and military equipment to the Third World." [43]

ZIONISM DECLARED RACISM

The union of the Third World with the Arabs was graphically demonstrated when Zionism was accused of being synonymous with racism. In a vote forced upon the United Nations, the Arabs united the Third World behind their nefarious charge and voted in a lie.

On the Zionism issue, 72 nations voted for the resolution and

35 voted against it. Of those voting for the racist charge, 58 were governments run by either dictatorships, strong men, or elite groups. It was virtually a case of elite dictatorships versus democracies. Vital in the prophetic pattern is that 23 of the negative votes were from black African nations. There are many reasons why so many of the Third World nations voted against Israel.

I believe a news magazine was correct when it said, "Arab nations have had little trouble lining up support among have-not countries for their anti-Israel campaign with promises of financial assistance or by threats of economic reprisals." [44]

MURDERERS HONORED AT U.N.

Two men honored at the U.N. as chiefs of state are both murderers and vicious plotters of the destruction of the Jewish state: Yassar Arafat, leader of the P.L.O. which has instigated terrorist actions in many countries; and Idi Amin, head of Uganda, who seized power in 1971 and has seen anywhere from 25,000 to 250,000 Ugandans murdered since then.

No one could have been more arrogantly and openly vicious than Amin as he spoke before the U.N. General Assembly and called for the extinction of Israel as a state. These words take on a very ominous tone to those who know of the Bible prophecies which link black African countries with the Arabs in a great final attack on Israel which will bring the Russians and finally all nations into the war.

The timetable of the prophetic countdown toward Armageddon is accelerating with these developments.

RED CHINA AND ASIA

Not only has the Arab-African sphere of power developed and fit into the prophetic scenario of the events leading to the Messiah's return, but Red China is beginning to pull together another predicted sphere of power.

According to the prophecy of the Book of Revelation concerning an awesome invasion of the Middle East by the Orientals in the last war, the Kings of the East will cross the Euphrates River and move westward with an army of 200 million soldiers. On the basis of this prophecy, I believe that Red China, which already boasts of a militia of 200 million, will gather around it some kind of confederacy including most of the nations of Asia, especially Japan.

THE GREAT ANTIHEGEMONY HOAX

Recent events are rapidly fitting into this prophetic pattern. Communist China is seeking to pull off one of the most clever political maneuvers to date. Using a treaty signed with Richard Nixon in 1972 which is called the *antihegemony agreement,* Red China is seeking to exploit this concept to bring virtually all of the non-Communist Asian countries into a mutual defense pact.

Red China desperately fears that Moscow and Hanoi will seek to impose their rule (hegemony) over more countries in Asia. (And their fears are well based.) This bothers Red China greatly —not because it wants to preserve the independence and freedom of these nations—but because it wants to take them over itself and yet is not quite prepared to do so.

It's been interesting to watch the grand hypocrisy of the Chinese Communists as they wine and dine American presidents and dignitaries and keep pressing for strong affirmations of U.S. commitment to the antihegemony treaty. The Chinese are adroitly using U.S. power to attempt to block further Russian conquest in Asia until they can do it themselves. The pity is we seem to be playing along with the whole obvious scheme.

THE KINGS OF THE EAST

The *Los Angeles Times* comments on China's purposes: "Communist China is seeking to mold the non-Communist nations of Asia into a mutual defense association aimed initially at Moscow and Hanoi. The alliance is further designed as the politicomilitary basis of a new world power bloc that Peking seeks, which would start with economic cooperation among Southeast Asia's non-communist countries." [45]

Not only is China pressing Japan for a mutual defense treaty, but they are now seeking to put together a mini-Asian Common Market which they aim to link up to the European Common Market. According to the Chinese Communist leaders, this is the first step toward an even grander world-power scheme.

"Peking, senior diplomats report, envisions the security alliance as a major, functioning force in international affairs by the 1990s. It would supplement and support the proposed basically economic association made up of the world's raw-material-producing nations as well as China, Japan, and Western Europe, a grouping which Peking envisions as the dominant force in the world by that time." [46]

The Red Chinese are moving toward the above alliance so that this bloc of power will push the United States and the Russian confederacy into secondary roles of economic power and start them on the decline as dominant military powers in the world.

If Red China can harness the Third World countries which have most of the world's raw materials under her leadership, it can force, if necessary, the European Common Market into a dynamic politicoeconomic and politicomilitary union with itself.

ANOTHER PROPHETIC RIDDLE CLEARS

The prophetic significance of the above developments are many. The first and most intriguing is that such a treaty as that being sought between Red China and the so-called raw-material-producing nations would explain why the Apostle John predicts the great army from the East will be attacking the Russians when they invade the Arab countries. (Daniel 11:40–45, Revelation 16:12.) This was discussed in great detail in *The Late Great Planet Earth,* chapter 12.

Second, it could also explain the way in which all the nations of the world are brought under the temporary control of the Dictator (Antichrist) of the Revived Roman Empire. Revelation 13:8 indicates that all who dwell on earth will follow this Roman dictator and Revelation 18 reveals that this person will control through a vast worldwide economic power base.

All of the above elements are part of the groundwork which China is unwittingly striving to lay.

Third, the pulling of Asian countries into an alliance with China would explain why John uses the plural, *Kings of the East,* when he predicts their invasion into the Middle East in the last war. It's of particular significance that under the provisions of the anti-hegemony agreement, an attack by Russia or any treaty country calls for an immediate military response by all, which is exactly what is predicted will happen in the biblical scenario.

The predicted events are falling together so quickly that the only logical conclusion is that Messiah's return cannot be too far away!

Where is America? In recent China relationships, no country has ever cooperated so naively in its own destruction as the USA. Unless American citizens can become aroused to influence their elected leaders, the direction of compromise and cooperation with the powers which would destroy America will continue unabated.

TIME MAGAZINE AND JESUS' PREDICTIONS

When a popular magazine features in its cover stories some phenomena which Jesus predicted would increase in frequency and magnitude like *birth pangs* it would seem that the secular press might be called the prophetic press.

Look at *Time* magazine. Within a comparatively short period of time it had cover story features on "Famine" (November 11, 1974), on "Forecast: Earthquakes" (September 1, 1975), on "The Crime Wave" (June 30, 1975), on the dangers of the uncontrolled arms race in relation to wars (February 11, 1974) and on false religion (October 13, 1975).

There has been an amazing and rapid acceleration in these prophetic signs which Jesus said would herald His soon return. He called these signs *birth pangs* and that is the key to understanding their significance. (*See* Matthew 24:4–12.) Just as a woman has severe pains which increase in frequency and intensity as the baby is about to be born, so the world will experience the birth pangs described by *Time* as time draws near for the birth of a new age which will follow Messiah Jesus' return.

BIRTH PANGS

Jesus began His discourse on signs which would precede His return by warning of false Christs and false prophets, of a great wave of counterfeit religion. We will explore these in depth in the next two chapters, since the false religion revival is sweeping in with a force unparalleled in history.

Jesus said that there will be an increase in famines. Famines have existed from time to time throughout history; however, the great famines of history will begin to develop simultaneously with all the other birth pangs.

Is this happening? Let's examine this dread specter. In 1967 two scientist brothers, William and Paul Paddock, wrote a book which few took seriously at the time. It was entitled *Famine Nineteen Seventy Five!* With the unemotional logic of facts and statistics they convincingly stated their proposition that 1975 would be the year in which an ever-accelerating age of famines would begin. They were wrong. The age of famines officially began in 1974. The geometrically increasing population working against a limited food supply, made even shorter by shifting weather patterns and oil-fertilizer supply shortages, brought about famines as they predicted.

Experts recognize that what we are witnessing today is unique. An article in the *New York Times* said: "With growing frequency, a variety of leading individual experts and relevant organizations are coming forth to warn that a major global food shortage is developing." [47]

Let's face it, no other generation in history has had to face the *addition* of 3.5 billion people to the population in less than twenty-five years. Yet this is what has been projected for population growth by the year 2000. [47a]

When we face the fact that we are already in desperate trouble with just over 4 billion on earth, what will happen with all the new arrivals?

In 1974 it was reported that "nearly half a billion people are suffering from some form of hunger; 10,000 of them die of starvation each week in Africa, Asia, and Latin America . . . ." [48]

The threat of famine is so great that several scientists, including author William Paddock, purchased a page in the *Wall Street Journal* to warn the U.S. Here are some of their urgent statements:

> Already sufficiently serious food crises have occurred in many of the developing countries to make it clear to all the "Time of Famines" has begun. This situation was accurately forecast a decade ago, but the prophets were denounced and ridiculed. It is now too late to prevent famines in the world . . . .[49]

EARTHQUAKES . . . WATCH OUT FOR THE JUPITER EFFECT

Another birth pang which Jesus said would signal His return would be the increase in frequency and magnitude of earthquakes. This phenomenon of nature is one of the most fearful that man has experienced down through history.

The power unleashed in an earthquake is almost incomprehensible. Scientists estimate that the energy released in the 1964 Alaskan quake was equal to several powerful hydrogen bombs. This quake had an 8.4 reading on the Richter scale, which is one of the strongest ever measured.

A great deal of research has been focused lately on the cause of quakes; the goal is to be able to forecast accurately when and where they will strike. One thing has become very clear as a result of this study and that is that earthquakes are increasing in frequency and intensity; they are beginning to occur in places previously unaffected.

The historical danger of quakes is that: "During recorded history, earthquakes—and the floods, fires and landslides they have triggered—are estimated to have taken as many as 74 million lives." [50]

In the same article, the greatest earthquakes known in history were listed. It was remarkable to note that of the fourteen greatest quakes known, nine of them have happened in the 20th century and five since 1960.

As this chapter was being written a massive earthquake (7.5 on the Richter scale) struck Guatemala, killing thousands and making hundreds of thousands homeless. This took only 39 seconds, and yet it was an eternity of terror.

Based on biblical prophecy, I believe that there will continue to be an increase in major earthquakes. (These things are not easy to write!)

In a recent book called *The Jupiter Effect*, written by two astronomers, John Gribbin and Stephen Plagemann, amazing things are being predicted to occur in 1982. The phenomenon they call the *Jupiter effect* is a rare planetary lineup which occurs every 179 years. All of the planets of this solar system become lined up in straight line perpendicular to the sun. According to Gribbin and Plagemann, the combined gravitational pull on one side of the sun could cause large storms on the sun which in turn, they believe, will produce the following effects: it will severely affect the upper parts of the earth's atmosphere, disturbing radio communications and unleashing an unusual display of the Northern lights. Global weather patterns will be greatly disrupted by radically altered wind directions in the upper atmosphere.

Another result of the Jupiter effect, according to Gribbin and Plagemann, will be that the earth's rotation will slow down causing significantly large enough stress on the great fault lines of our planet that great earthquakes will be triggered.[50a]

Some experts disagree with these projected results; however, if the authors are correct, then the accelerated pace of earthquakes and changing weather patterns would be greatly intensified.

WEATHER PATTERN CHANGES

Whether the Jupiter effect theory is correct or not, because of the clear pattern of events predicted in the Bible, I believe we should anticipate a great increase in unusual weather changes.

Some of these weather patterns are described in the following prophecies:

Jesus forecast of this time that there will be ". . . fearful events and great signs from heaven" (Luke 21:11 NIV). And again, "There will be signs in the sun, moon and stars . . . nations will be in anguish and perplexity at the roaring and tossing of the sea. Men will faint from terror, apprehensive of what is coming on the world, for the heavenly bodies will be shaken" (Luke 21:25, 26 NIV).

This sounds like some kind of radical astrological upheaval, probably occurring first on the sun, then affecting the other heavenly bodies of our solar system. Jesus' prediction links this to terrifying storms upon the planet's oceans.

All of this cause and effect fits into the pattern that our growing scientific knowledge reveals.

PREDICTIONS FROM UNPREDICTABLE SOURCES

More and more people are becoming interested in Bible prophecy, not just as a whim, but as a verification of events in the world today. Scientists, psychologists, sociologists, and educators who might not believe in the Bible as the source of truth, are making the same predictions as those of the ancient prophets!

We have seen significant changes on the world scene, even in the past five years: Arab power; Israel's deteriorating position; alignment of the Third World with the Arabs; an avalanche of crime and lawlessness; China's attempt to unify Asian countries behind it; famine, earthquakes, weapons of war; move toward one-worldism; decline of morality; increase in the occult.

As an individual looks for a way to cope with life—as he searches for hope in what appears to be a hopeless world—many are helpless. In this state, there are many false hopes and false prophets waiting to occupy the void in empty lives.

How discerning we must be! As Jesus has warned, "For false Christs and false prophets will arise and will show great signs and wonders, so as to mislead, if possible, even the elect" (Matthew 24:24).

How alert we should be! When I see all these events coming together simultaneously I feel like shouting, "Wake up, World, Jesus is almost here!"

Truth stands the test of time; lies are soon exposed.

Proverbs 12:19 LB

5

False Hopes

The despair of this age is driving men and women to search for hope through many avenues. Where is the hope anticipated by the promises of the past generation? Where is the New Deal, the Great Society, the renewal, the recycling, or all the other solemn pledges given by sincere men? The problems remain. The Age of Aquarius has not ushered in utopia.

There was another era in our not-too-distant past which was a harbinger of today. Circumstances were similar and the directions were the same. Fifty years ago, before the reign of Hitler, there was a buildup of stress which gives us today an ominous indication of the way in which history repeats itself.

In Berlin during the 1920s drugs were so widely used that cocaine was called the basic drug of the city. Cocaine was everywhere. ". . . Girls pushed it in nightclubs, one-legged war veterans sold it on street corners, and if one were going on a trip, everybody knew of foreign contacts . . . ." [51]

Morphine was almost as widely used as cocaine. Hermann Goering, one of Hitler's right-hand men and commander of the *Luftwaffe*, was an addict. One actress was quoted as saying that the reason for so many addicts was because of "the horrible life" in Germany at that time.

What were some of the contributing factors to that "horrible life"? In the early 1930s it was obvious that Germany was engulfed in an economic crisis of gigantic proportion. At the same time the greatest prosperity was being enjoyed by clairvoyants and soothsayers. The occult was having a heyday! Newsstands were filled with astrology articles and columns; mediums were enjoying so much prominence that they had posh offices and kept regular business hours. It was said of one of these businessmen mediums:

. . . The most celebrated of these was a short, swarthy Viennese named Herschel Steinschneider. A former journalist, who also dabbled in blackmail, he had once written several pamphlets exposing fortune-tellers but then decided that there was more money to be made by joining them . . . .[52]

Naturally, if you can't fight 'em . . . .

Economically Germany was so unstable that city governments defaulted on their bonds, small businesses failed rapidly, and industrial production plummeted.

As the nation of Germany was caught in what seemed a hopeless situation, one famous philosopher-historian wrote that what Germany needed was a strong man. Oswald Spengler, the influential author of *Decline of the West*, said in the 1920s, "We must go right through to the end of our misfortune; we need a chastisement compared to which the four years of war are nothing . . . . A dictatorship, resembling that of Napoleon, will be regarded universally as salvation. But then blood must flow, the more the better . . . ."[53]

Hitler did not take over Germany by force; he was actually voted into power and could claim his right to become Chancellor by constitutional means.

Many Germans were stunned by the victory of the strange little man with the fanatical eyes and shrill voice, but they had little idea of the demonic ideas which would drive the Führer to the disastrous results of his insane rule.

One young intellectual wrote: "Seldom has a nation so readily surrendered all its rights and liberties as did ours in those first hopeful, intoxicated months of the new millennium . . . . The lost war, continual unrest, the inflation, grave evidences of cultural decay, unemployment . . . all these things and a great deal more preyed upon the souls of sixty million people. And then it suddenly appeared that the pressure was relaxing . . . ."[54]

The way had been prepared in Germany for the false hope of a savior—a strong man. The despair which had been building to such a crescendo found relief in anyone who would provide direction.

Does any of this have a familiar ring? There was Germany in the twenties and thirties—extreme drug usage, increase in the occult, cities in a financial bind and going broke, inflation, an undercurrent of unrest among the populace. Germany forty or fifty years ago was a mirror of the United States in the 1970s.

Just as people searched for hope in pre-Hitler Germany, and reached the place where the desire for strong leadership was so prevalent that a man like Hitler was voted into power, so the world is grabbing for false hopes today.

The present growing crises and despair are fitting into the predicted conditions which the Bible said would bring in a worldwide acceptance of a totalitarian one-world government and the great global dictator which God calls the Antichrist.

What Germany experienced on a national scale is now sweeping upon us on a global scale, only with even more dreadful dimensions. We know the Germans experienced national economic chaos; however there were certain parts of their culture which gave them some sense of security. Family structure was fairly solid, right and wrong had limits. Although the shock of a depressed economy was severe, it wasn't totally hopeless.

Best-selling author Alvin Toffler says of this period, "The world of the 1920's was a much simpler place in which individuals, even if hungry and jobless, knew more or less where they stood in the scheme of things. This is no longer true. Millions are overwhelmed by uncertainty, identities fragmented and loyalties confused and self-cancelling." [55]

Toffler's book *The Eco-Spasm Report* is a fearful prediction of a global economic disaster possibly within this decade which will only be solved by bringing in a "new world order" with some form of global government and world-economic control.

This secular prophet describes eco-spasm as follows:

> Indeed, what we are seeing today is not simply an *economic* upheaval, but something far deeper, something that cannot be understood within the framework of conventional economics . . . .
>
> What we are seeing is . . . a crisis that is simultaneously tearing up our energy base, our value systems, our family structures, our institutions, our communicative modes, our sense of space and time and our epistemology as well as our economy. What is happening . . . is the breakdown of industrial civilization . . . and the first fragmentary appearance of a wholly new . . . social

order: a super-industrial civilization that will be technological, but no longer industrial.[56]

Although Toffler may not realize it, what he has predicted is what Bible prophecy describes. The great one-world government which will be established just before the return of Jesus the Messiah is based upon an economic structure.

In the Book of Revelation the final destruction of this satanically controlled system is described. When the capital of the world empire is destroyed, the men who control the wealth—the merchants of the earth—will be in the worst state of despair. This future world event will make the Wall Street crash of the 1920s look like John Paul Getty's losing a penny.

As they watch their fortunes turned to rubble, listen to their lament:

> The merchants of the earth will weep and mourn over her because no one buys their cargoes any more—cargoes of gold, silver, precious stones and pearls; fine linen, purple, silk and scarlet cloth; every sort of citron wood, and articles of every kind made of ivory, costly wood, bronze, iron and marble; cargoes of cinnamon and spice, of incense, myrrh and frankincense, of wine and olive oil, of fine flour and wheat; cattle and sheep; horses and carriages; and bodies and souls of men.
>
> They will say, "The fruit you longed for is gone from you. All your riches and splendor have vanished, never to be recovered." The merchants who sold these things and gained their wealth from her will stand far off, terrified at her torment. They will weep and mourn and cry out:
>
> "Woe! Woe, O great city,
>   dressed in fine linen, purple and scarlet,
>   and glittering with gold, precious stones and pearls!
>   In one hour such great wealth has been
>   brought to ruin!"
>
> Every sea captain, and all who travel by ship, the sailors, and all who earn their living from the sea, will stand far off. When they see the smoke of her burning, they will exclaim, "Was there

ever a city like this great city?" They will throw dust on their heads, and with weeping and mourning cry out. . . .

Revelation 18:11–19 NIV

Economic crises are driving the world toward one-worldism, but there is another factor accelerating the push in the same direction. That is the multiplication of nuclear weapons in more and more countries.

This threat is so great that five nuclear arms experts from Harvard and M.I.T. recently warned, "A very nasty kind of world government may be the only way to keep the world from blowing itself up in a nuclear war."

The experts continued to say about the war threat, "A nuclear war probably would not originate with the United States or the Soviet Union, but with relatively smaller nations like Israel, its Arab neighbors, India, Pakistan or some African country." [57]

A Princeton professor published a comprehensive work on the arms race and was quoted as saying that "The only way to solve the problem may be some form of world government." [58]

A professor of international relations writes: ". . . Visions of the future conjure up a world without borders, a world village, and a global shopping center, thus providing us with contemporary versions of world federalism, world government, and world rule through world law." [59]

In its conference in Nairobi, Kenya, in the latter part of 1975 the World Council of Churches drafted some proposals for a "new world economic and social order and warned that the world could destroy itself within a generation unless wide-ranging changes were made." [60]

Arnold Toynbee, one of the greatest historians of all time, said, "One of the most conspicuous marks of disintegration of a society is when it purchases a reprieve by submitting to forcible political unification in a universal state." [61]

Headlines like these literally leap out at the person who knows biblical prophecy. What do we read into this trend in world affairs? A world which is terrified at the thought of war will welcome with open arms and relieved sighs the Antichrist and his ingenious leadership. The Bible says, ". . . The whole world was

astonished and followed the beast [the Antichrist]. Men worshiped the dragon [Satan] because he had given authority to the
beast, and they also worshiped the beast and asked, 'Who is like
the beast? Who can make war against him?' " (Revelation 13:3, 4
NIV).

The cry of the world, "Who can make war against him [the
Antichrist]?" shows that war seems to be the world's greatest fear
and that the Antichrist somehow brings in a system that will seem
to end the threat of war for all times.

As I see all these things fitting exactly into the whole prophetic
pattern, I am personally electrified by two things: (1) that this
is the general time of Jesus' return; and (2) I will have a good
chance of being part of that incredibly privileged group who will
suddenly meet the Lord and bypass physical death.

For false [Messiahs] and false prophets will arise and will show great signs and wonders, so as to mislead, if possible, even the elect.

JESUS THE MESSIAH
in Matthew 24:24

6

False Prophets

Rudyard Kipling wrote over eighty-five years ago:

Oh, East is East, and West is West, and never the twain shall meet,
Till Earth and Sky stand presently at God's great Judgment Seat.

I can't help wondering how astonished Kipling might be to see how the East and the West are meeting today.

In the space of one day this was graphically revealed to me. It began when I went to have my picture taken. The young photographer was engrossed in a book on Vedic revelation. A little while later as I left on a trip I noted that the girl at the airline check-out counter was studying the writings of some guru. After I got my ticket I was confronted in the airport lounge by a man in a long saffron robe, offering me still another Eastern religious tract.

In the Western world—and in the United States in particular—there is an unprecedented rush into Eastern religions. The young, the intellectual, the businessman, the housewife are becoming a part of a type of thinking which was alien to the America of a decade ago.

Just as nations are being pushed toward one-world government and the Antichrist, so individuals are being pulled toward false prophets.

It seems that people are willing to follow anything or anyone if there is a hope of peace!

INTO TM

The quest for a tranquil spirit in the midst of a tumultuous world has led many people into what its leader calls a "natural, simple technique" called *Transcendental Meditation*. The Indian guru who heads this movement is Maharishi Mahesh Yogi and he

77

recently told a well-known television interviewer that TM is "the greatest fulfillment for all mankind." [62]

According to *Time* magazine, TM is the "turn-on of the '70's— a drugless high that even the narc squad might enjoy . . . ." [63]

With its rapid increase, its frank goals for reaching the entire population of America, and its acceptance by so many prominent persons, it is certainly reaching a large audience.

The *Los Angeles Times* calls it "the fastest growing cult in the West." [64]

What is TM?

TM is a system of Hindu yoga in which the initiate meditates twice daily on a *mantra*, which is a Hindu word derived from their Vedic literature.

Those involved in TM are more adamant about what TM isn't, rather than what it is. They say it is not a religion; they claim that it is a method to relieve stress. They point to people in the entertainment field, sports, politics, and business who are TM advocates and who respond to questions with glowing testimonies.

One of the main reasons I believe it is important to disclose the true nature of TM is that we know many people who have become innocently involved in it, only to realize that it is a deceptive angel of light.

The impact of TM in the United States is amazing in the number of its initiates and the rapidity of its influence. TM is being taught in hundreds of public schools throughout the U.S., from the junior-high to the university level. The state legislatures of Illinois and Connecticut have passed resolutions urging the teaching of TM in public schools. The TM movement is the umbrella for different organizations, all coordinated by the World Plan Executive Council. The Students International Meditation Society is for students and youth; the International Meditation Society, designed for adults; the Spiritual Regeneration Movement, originally for retired people, but now for anyone interested in spiritual emphasis; the Foundation of the Science of Creative Intelligence, for business, industry and management; the Maharishi International University in Fairfield, Iowa, for relating TM to all disciplines of knowledge.[64a]

TM is having a wide political impact. Many state legislators as well as U.S. Congressmen are advocates. Philip Ferguson, research coordinator of TM's International Center for Scientific Research stated: "There are a couple of strong contenders for the Presidency—very strong—who practice TM." [65]

A comprehensive study of TM done by a team of researchers in Berkeley, California, contains a provocative statement. It reveals that the central problem with TM is that it "fails to introduce us to the One who is the source of our morality; it names, instead, an abstract, extended version of ourselves as the origin of ourselves and of our conscience." [66]

Although the Maharishi stated on the Merv Griffin show that TM is not a religion, he writes in the *Meditations of the Maharishi,* a book for TM instructors, "Transcendental Meditation is a path to God" (page 59).

He also says in *Transcendental Meditation,* page 253, that "The fulfillment of every religion is the simple practice of transcendental deep meditation."

The Maharishi himself was commissioned to develop God-realization for the masses by the Hindu, Swami Brahamananda Saraswati, one of the four major religious leaders in India at one time. The initiation ceremony of TM is in the classic Hindu format, including giving the initiate the secret mantra, which is the Sanskrit word used in Hindu meditation.

Maharishi speaks of "God-consciousness," as well as a level known as "Brahman-consciousness." "Brahman" is the name given to the impersonal, final absolute Reality—the supreme god of Hinduism.

How, then, can they make the claim that TM is not a religion?

The nonreligious facade of TM is one of the deceptions of false prophets which is being swallowed by Westerners. The Maharishi was questioned by a reporter from the *San Francisco Chronicle,* March 29, 1975, in which the reporter asked this question:

REPORTER   Haven't you been downplaying the spiritual nature of TM in order to attract more businessmen?

MAHARISHI   I'm not downplaying it. It's only that I'm not talking about it.

It becomes quite obvious that the religious nature of TM poses serious problems when legislators advocate it, when resolutions are passed recommending its practices, and when our tax-supported institutions are offering courses in it.

Many persons might not be concerned from the standpoint of whether or not TM is a religious practice. However, there are increasing cases of the mental and psychological danger.

Here is what psychiatrists are saying: ". . . the TM organization does not screen prospective meditators and that the technique —especially a sequence of extra meditations called 'rounding'— might well cause unstable persons to go over the edge." [67]

Here in America the cultural and political environment have set the stage for another TM deception. Maharishi and his followers are obviously on a world crusade for their cause. Why? Are they aiming to evangelize the world into relaxation?

An excerpt from a publication of the Maharishi International University was very revealing. Dr. Stanley Kater of the Neurobiology Department of the university had this exchange in an interview with Maharishi:

DR. KATER   You see, you have to be fit to survive, and the many follow the few who show the many the way to be fit—it is the law that the rest will follow, or they will be unfit.

MAHARISHI   Very beautiful. There has not been and there will not be a place for the unfit. The fit will lead, and if the unfit are not coming along there is no place for them . . . in the Age of Enlightenment there is no place for ignorant people. The ignorant will be made enlightened by a few orderly, enlightened people moving around. [68]

I am deeply concerned for those who innocently follow the false prophets in such movements as TM. Other cults will appear and fade, be revealed as frauds and fall into disfavor, but as long as man does not know the true and only hope, he will continue to follow these deceptions.

WHAT IS EST?

We were attending some classes at a California State University when several students and teachers mentioned a man by the name of Werner Erhard and a program called est. At first I thought they were talking about extrasensory perception, but soon learned that this was entirely different and another movement which is far more widespread than I thought.

Erhard is one of the leading spokesmen in the area of "human consciousness." One of the reasons it is not as well known as TM, Scientology, or some of the other cultic movements is because Erhard himself has said that he has avoided publicity or media coverage because he wanted people to know about est either as a direct experience or as a communication from someone who had the direct experience.

Many new movements, like est, are for the purpose of "realizing the human potential," as Erhard explains. It is a "search for a new way of being." Erhard attempts to describe est, which is difficult even for its founder, because it is based so much on individual experience. He says, "We're not trying to get people to take responsibility for their history, although that seems to be another result. What we think happens is that people go beyond emotion, attitude and body sensation, to a thing we call experience. Experience for us has no form to it; it's pure substance without any form." [68a]

The founder of est is a man who gives a great deal of credit to his association with Scientology, which is another worldwide movement whose leader, L. Ron Hubbard, describes his self-styled religion as "the most vital movement on Earth today."

Erhard considers L. Ron Hubbard a genius, but decided to leave the Church of Scientology to establish his own training.

Those who have taken est training have revealing reactions: "Est training points out that your life isn't working." "It was exquisitely boring. Nothing to do but experience your experience." [68b]

Another est trainee said, "I see Werner as a revolutionary shaking up peoples' pasts and pushing them into the future . . . est is an important part of the *Easternization* of America." [69]

Maharishi, Erhard, Hubbard, and many others. Examine carefully the leaders of some of these movements. This is an important determination we must make for ourselves and questions we should ask of those who get caught in these movements. What are the motivations and aims of these men?

OH, MR. MOON!

" 'I will conquer and subjugate the world,' says Sun Myung Moon. 'I am your brain.' " [70]

Moon is a South Korean who established the Unification Church, took large ads in leading newspapers, and proceeded to gather his disciples by the thousands. He might not be taken as seriously as Scientology or TM except that his particular brand of Christian cultism is appealing to many young people who are lonely and searching for love and identity in an impersonal world.

Moon's young American converts regard him as the second Christ. With his own brand of teaching from the prophetic Scriptures, a strong dose of anticommunism and American flag-waving, Moon has mesmerized his followers. Many parents are heartsick over their sons and daughters who have abandoned their own families, their ambitions, and their material possessions to follow the self-styled messiah. "Moon converts seem to have had little attachment to other religions and appear to be grasping for a sense of stability and morality . . . ." [71]

An example of the psychological conditioning exerted by the Unification Church came to my attention. An English girl in her twenties came to America and was staying with friends in Los Angeles. Brenda was looking for a job—lonely and discouraged—when a young woman about her own age stopped her on Wilshire Boulevard and began to talk to her. Brenda was delighted with a word of hope, with someone who took some interest in her. She was told about this marvelous church where everyone felt part of a real family, and she decided to go.

Brenda became a part of Moon's followers. She turned over what little money and possessions she had to the "family," because everyone shared equally. Her sense of morality seemed heightened because the ideals which were preached appealed to the basic desire of youth to build a better world.

A friend of mine spent time with Brenda and patiently showed her from the Bible the fallacy of what she had been learning. Slowly, Brenda realized that Moon was not the messiah, but it was obvious that the influence of his camps, his church, and his teachings had affected her strongly.

In the latter part of 1975 the cult was growing strongly and its members believe that Moon is a "Lord of the Second Advent."

As Jesus warned of the signs of the end-times, He made more statements about false religions and false messiahs than any other. "Watch out that no one deceives you. For many will come in my name, claiming, 'I am the Christ,' and will deceive many" (Matthew 24:4, 5 NIV).

WHAT NEXT? A NEW WORLD VIEW

As man's search for new experiences, new leaders, new hopes, increases in intensity, there will be that continued desire to find an alternative route into what appears to be a dark future.

We come to another turn. Out of the philosophical views of the past, into the predictable results in modern society, comes something called the *New Consciousness*. Some of this new way of expression and understanding is still in the embryonic stage; some is taking form in ways which only the most discerning will be able to uncover.

One of the difficulties in understanding this trend of thought is that the scholars and writers who are the participants aren't sure themselves what they mean. Just as the people who participated in est found it difficult to describe their experience within the context of language, so many of the proponents of the New Consciousness find themselves limited. However, if we analyze some of the directions these mind-molders are taking, we discover certain terms which they have in common and a pattern which gallops through their corral of ideas.

Words to quiver our antenna are: *consciousness change, humanistic experience, beingness, a new reality, the learning of enlightenment, peak experience,* and *human dynamics.*

Some of the leaders in what one writer calls The Newest Intellectual Fashion are Carlos Castaneda (anthropology), Robert Ornstein (psychology), Joe Kamiya (pioneer of bio-feedback training), Aldous Huxley (drug research), and George Leonard (sociology and cultural history).[72]

If the names and some of the concepts of these men seem remote to your personal life-style now, it would be wise to consider that whenever seeds are planted in the educational system or culture, the growth and consequences are soon spreading wide influence.

A few years ago I thought acupuncture had something to do with a flat tire. *Consciousness, beingness,* and *bliss* were terms tossed around by the ivory-tower boys in think tanks. Today, however, the New Consciousness (and I capitalize it because of the importance of the inroads it is making in modern thought) is developing a new vocabulary for this accelerated age.

There seems to be a theme and a certain progression in the different advocates of the new world view. As we describe some of its leading exponents see if you can pick out the common denominator.

NEW CONSCIOUSNESS: THE ANTHROPOLOGIST

A few years ago when I first heard of Carlos Castaneda on the campus at UCLA I realized that this young anthropologist had a thesis and an appeal which would grab students. I didn't realize in the early 1970s the national impact he would have. Castaneda began in 1968 with a book which was his master's thesis, *The Teachings of Don Juan,* and then followed that up with sequels which made himself and the subject of his writings cult figures in the United States at a time when the nature of our generation is demanding a belief in something. Castaneda's books are stories of how a young scholar became involved in the practice of Indian sorcery through a wily old Mexican by the name of Don Juan. Drugs and sorcery are woven into experiences with unreal explanations.

What are some of these teachings of Don Juan? "Don Juan's teachings have reached print at precisely the moment when more Americans than ever before are disposed to consider 'non-rational' approaches to reality." [73]

Don Juan (and there are conflicting opinions on whether he is alive and well or a vivid figment of Castaneda's imagination) advocates certain drugs which give him access to powers and forces that a "man of knowledge" must use.

"The learning of enlightenment is a common theme in the favorite reading of young Americans today." Because of this trend, many have been excited about Castaneda's experience-teaching, even when they do not understand quite what he means. One commentator referred to his books as ". . . an alternative to both the guilt-ridden Judaeo-Christian and the blindly mechanistic views of man . . . . Don Juan's way regards man as central and important. By not separating ourselves from nature, we return to a position of dignity." [74]

NEW CONSCIOUSNESS: THE SCIENTIST

The new thought extends into the scientific world. Dr. Robert E. Ornstein is a young researcher at the Langley Porter Neuro-psychiatric Institute in San Francisco. He spoke at the American Association for the Advancement of Science and drew a gigantic crowd where "Not only scientists but philosophy students and yoga practitioners are drawn to hear him because of his venturesome effort to reunite science and spirit, reason and intuition." [75]

Basically, what Ornstein desires is a marriage of the techniques of the scientific lab with the concerns of the mystics. He advocates a return to a stronger concern with consciousness and sub-consciousness, which has led him personally to Zen and the I Ching.

The influence of Ornstein is not to be underestimated. His book *The Psychology of Consciousness*, which was published in 1973, is being used by more than 300 colleges and universities in many departments, ranging from biology to religion.

Another influential pioneer of the new thought is Joe Kamiya, a pioneer of bio-feedback training. Great expectations were raised in this field, which was once called the greatest development in the history of psychology. Kamiya was said to believe that "people will soon control phobias and anxieties." [76]

It was reported, however, that the "inflated hopes for bio-feedback may have been related to the growth of interest in Eastern mysticism. Glowingly described by fans as 'electronic yoga,' bio-feedback seemed to offer inner exploration without drugs, religion or psychotherapy . . . ." [77]

NEW CONSCIOUSNESS: THE RESEARCHER

In drug research probably one of the most influential thinkers and writers has been Aldous Huxley. As he describes the experience of using mescalin, it is a desirable state, more ideal than the alcohol, marijuana, barbiturate culture which is so predominant. Huxley has the attitude of an idealist who is wishing for the substitution of old bad habits for new and less harmful ones. He says, "A man under the influence of mescalin quietly minds his own business. Moreover, the business he minds is an experience of the most enlightening kind . . . ." [78]

Most important, Huxley is advocating that it is vital to be "shaken out of the ruts of ordinary perception, to be shown for a few timeless hours the outer and the inner world . . . this is an experience of inestimable value to everyone and especially to the intellectual . . . ." [79]

NEW CONSCIOUSNESS: THE SCHOLAR

George Leonard attempts to explain the language of the New Consciousness, but bogs down as he says that ". . . we have no standard, acceptable vocabulary of consciousness change." As a scholar concerned with the inadequacy of mere language in describing experience, he says, ". . . But we do need the encyclopedic spirit, something like a comprehensive 'instruction in the circle of arts and science' for an age of transformation of consciousness. Perhaps it has already begun, not just in books and papers and seminars but also in tapes, films, and videotapes, for there are many authors, thinkers, and adventurers today who are concerned, in sometimes separate ways, with being and transformation . . . ." [80]

In the next few years this educational and philosophical trend is going to become more and more noticeable. At the core of the belief (or nonbelief, however you wish to interpret it) is *Man*. Some of the writings use the capitalization of that word to emphasize that Man is the universal center. The second important issue is that the universe we live in is both visible and invisible and that through the invisible universe we are able to become separate from reality and experience altered states of consciousness. In order to experience cosmic consciousness we become aware of both the visible and invisible, but there is no distinction between illusion and reality.

If all of this sounds rather nebulous it is because the New Consciousness is ". . . in the same state of formulation as deism in the late seventeenth century, or naturalism in the early eighteenth century. Intellectuals were then spinning out new ways of grasping reality, but in the minds of thinking people in general these new ways were fuzzy and ill-defined . . . ." [81]

FROM CULT TO CONSCIOUSNESS TO OCCULT

While many people pray for revival in America, there are others who realize that it is already here. However, it is the occult revival which is permeating Western society, taking many forms, providing a background for practices which have been alien to the culture of the twentieth century.

It has been estimated that $150 million a year is spent on horoscopes in America according to an article in the magazine *Intellect* (November, 1975). The commercial aspects of the occult have reached lucrative proportions with posters, T-shirts, cookbooks, and many other cultural trappings.

It's not just the uninformed or ignorant who are involved in the occult, either. An article in an intellectual journal stated, "The recent interest [in the occult] seems to stem precisely from that segment of society which is college-educated, middle-class and relatively affluent. These are the people who ought to know better!" [82]

Such a dramatic change in basic thinking has occurred that we have made the transition from the age of rationalism to a new age of supernaturalism, or as it is more respectfully called, *parapsychology* and *extrasensory perception*. The average secular man now accepts the possibility of such phenomena, whereas fifteen years ago he would have laughed at or rejected it.

Just how deep and dramatic the acceptance of the occult has been is illustrated by the following statement on higher education in *Fortune* magazine: ". . . as to rationality, an astonishing number of students now believe, or profess to believe, in the occult, witchcraft, astrology and the more simple-minded forms of mysticism . . . ." [83]

What I noted as a growing trend toward this in *The Late Great Planet Earth* and *Satan Is Alive and Well on Planet Earth* is now an established fact. I believe that the false prophets which were predicted in the days before the return of Jesus Christ are going to increase in influence and numbers. The emphasis upon man as the center of the universe, the influx of Eastern religions and cults, and the attention to the occult are preparing the world to accept the Antichrist who will come into world power largely through his occultic, supernatural powers.

The Bible prophetically warns of this dictator's real miracles performed in Satan's power: ". . . the one whose coming is in accord with the activity of Satan, with all power and signs and false wonders, and with all the deception of wickedness for those who perish, because they did not receive the love of the truth so as to be saved. And for this reason God will send upon them a deluding influence so that they might believe what is false" (2 Thessalonians 2:9–11).

Don't be a part of the vast crowd that will be deceived by the ingenious schemes of this coming world leader. If you are dabbling in various new cults and occultic sects you are already into what the Bible prophets call "the spirit of antichrist" (*see* 1 John 4:3). You are subtly being prepared to accept this counterfeit messiah when he comes.

The Antichrist will not appear to be evil. He will seem to be the answer to all the world's ills. He will have electrifying answers for the desperate crises that are now mounting. He will deceive all those who have not developed a love for the truth which is the Bible. This one who seems so good at first will bring about the most total enslavement of people ever seen on this earth. There will be no freedom even to think. George Orwell's book *1984* doesn't even describe the tyranny predicted of this time.

True hope is found only in the Word of God—the Bible. Take hold of its hope. It will not only give your life new excitement, motivation, and stability, but will protect you from the flood of false prophets that are now coming upon this generation.

. . . But hope that is seen is no hope at all. Who hopes for what he already has? But if we hope for what we do not yet have, we wait for it patiently.

PAUL to the Romans (8:24, 25 NIV)

7

Hope–Not Wishful Thinking

Hope is one of the most important words in life—it is imperative in everyday living. The Austrian psychiatrist, Dr. Viktor Frankl, a prisoner in bestial concentration camps for many years, demonstrated that a person doesn't continue to live very long physically after hope is lost. But even the slightest ray of hope—the rumor of better food—a whisper about an escape—caused people to continue living even under the systematic horror of Hitler's execution camps.[84]

Hope. This is the word—and its meaning to us—that we will examine.

The modern dictionary definition for hope is "to wish for," "to expect" (but without certainty), "to desire very much" (but with no real assurance of obtaining your desire).

Test this yourself—ask a student, "Did you pass your exam?" The answer will usually be, "I hope so."

I hope so is the expression of a wish or a desire. But in the Bible hope is an indication of certainty.

Biblical hope is first an attitude of faith in things we are promised for the future. Faith is something which we choose to have, issue by issue. Faith looks at something God says in the Bible, believes it's true, and then acts upon this truth.

Hope, on the other hand, is a deeper attitude which grows as faith counts God's promises true. This hope acts like an anchor to stabilize our lives in the present and give us meaning, direction, and optimism.

Isn't that the kind of hope we need?

If you think that word study is just an exercise in dry semantics, you may be in for a surprise. Years ago, as a young believer eager to understand how to appropriate God's promises for my life, I discovered the value of discovering the precision of word meanings. God never uses a shrug of His shoulders in giving us directions for living. The *y' knows* which stumble through our modern conversations are not a part of the beautiful accuracy of the Bible.

HOPE IN THE OLD TESTAMENT

The Hebrew language of the Old Testament is rich in words which mean *hope*. Each Hebrew word contributes a valuable insight into the many shades of meaning that are inherent in *hope*. Let's examine these words and see how words written thousands of years ago leap right into the twentieth century—and our lives.

QAVAH: HOPE THAT GIVES NEW STRENGTH

The original idea of this verb was *to twist or to stretch something*.[85] It was associated with the twisting and stretching of weak strands into a strong rope. From this the word metaphorically developed into the idea of enduring under tension. This concept sprung from the fact that even a weak thread twisted together with a rope became strong.

The belief grew that as we hope in the Lord's promises we are woven into His strength and strengthened to withstand the stresses of life.

A great promise given by Isaiah illustrates this word:

Yet those who WAIT for the Lord will gain new strength;
They will mount up with wings like eagles,
They will run and not get tired,
They will walk and not become weary.

Isaiah 40:31 (*italics mine*)

The word translated *wait* in Isaiah is *qavah*. The major shade of meaning in this is "waiting in the expectant HOPE and being strengthened thereby." The margin note renders it "who HOPE in the Lord," which is more accurate.

How rich the meaning is when it is related to the whole verse. God promises that "those who hope in the Lord" will gain new strength to face the tensions and stresses of life—our strength is woven into His mighty strength like the strand in a rope.

Just as a strand in a rope cannot be broken even under great stress, so those whose direction of hope is in God's promises of strength, deliverance and ultimate eternal life cannot be broken.

A sure hope in the future enables a person to have superhuman strength:

> He gives strength to the weary,
> And to him who lacks might He increases power.
> Though youths grow weary and tired,
> And vigorous young men stumble badly,
> Yet those who [HOPE in] the Lord
> Will gain new strength . . . .
> Isaiah 40:29–31

King David in writing the Psalms uses this word more frequently than any other biblical writer. This word actually was one of the keys to David's life. He recognized that his human strength was never enough to meet the stresses of life.

YACHAL: HOPE THAT GIVES ENDURANCE

The root idea of this word is to wait for something. It came to mean an expectant waiting under extreme pressure. The scholar R. B. Girdlestone says, "*Yachal* occurs several times in the Book of Job and signifies a long patient waiting." [86]

A study of the usage of this word in the Book of Job gives the most accurate connotations. Job was a man going through extreme trial: he lost his great wealth, all his children, and his health—in rapid succession. He was suffering incredible and constant physical and mental pain.

Yet as he thought of why God had permitted all this he says, "Though He [God] slay me, I will *HOPE* in Him" (Job 13:15). Here the word *yachal* means to keep on hoping with endurance under extreme pressure. Job's hope in the Lord enabled him to endure and be stabilized even under adverse conditions.

One of the reasons for Job's tenacious hope was his faith in God's promise of the resurrection of his body. Listen to the courage inspired by this hope, even though his body was disintegrating and wracked with pain. "For I know that my redeemer liveth, and that he shall stand at the latter day upon the earth: And though after my skin worms destroy this body, yet in my flesh shall I see God: Whom I shall see for myself, and mine eyes shall behold, and not another; though my [heart] be consumed within me" (Job 19:25-27 KJV). This verse expressed the content of his hope.

David the Psalmist brings out clearly the enduring and patient waiting aspect of this word when he says, "But as for me, I will *HOPE* continually, And will praise Thee yet more and more" (Psalms 71:14). David was fighting the anxiety both of getting old and being surrounded by enemies. Yet his hope in God's promises that He would never forsake him caused him to be stabilized and to endure.

One of the most powerful examples of *yachal* is in Lamentations. Jeremiah is expressing his deep grief over the devastation of his nation in this book. All that was familiar and comfortable—his people—the Temple of God—the city of Jerusalem, where so many sacred shrines and memories were—the nation itself—all were destroyed by the ruthless army of Babylon, who didn't even spare the women and children. Those who survived the holocaust were taken off naked and in chains.

How would you cope with something like this? Suppose, for instance, that the Russians and the Red Chinese invaded and destroyed the United States. Suppose all of the shrines that we hold dear in Washington, D.C., lay in rubble. Suppose all the churches were ravaged, the women and children violated. What would you do? Would you be able to take the example of Jeremiah as he says:

"This I recall to my mind, therefore have I HOPE. It is because of the LORD's mercies that we are not consumed, because his compassions fail not. They are new every morning: great is thy faithfulness. The LORD is my portion, saith my soul; therefore will I HOPE in him" (Lamentations 3:21-24 KJV).

We can see here that *yachal* is used in the sense of having a patient, expectant hope in God Himself and realizing that the only reason the whole nation and all of its people weren't totally consumed was because of the Lord's mercies.

Jeremiah found that the Lord's compassion was renewed in him every day and he said that the whole foundation of what sustained him in that dark hour was that God's faithfulness is new every morning.

As Jeremiah looked at all this devastation and was tempted to lose all orientation to life, he said that his portion wasn't the Temple or the people or the nation—but his portion was the Lord Himself and that's why he had hope.

I think that this beautifully illustrates the word *yachal*, which means to be strengthened under stress and focus on the object of hope which is God Himself.

If this is the Terminal Generation, then we certainly need to have this kind of hope. We need to learn from the promises of the Word of God and from the examples of God's character that He is faithful in every situation. We need to draw strength from that kind of hope.

This is not an exercise in fear, or a practice in doomsmanship. No country or people can be complacent in our times. Disaster and devastation worse than that of Jeremiah's age could happen here.

BATACH: HOPE THAT INSPIRES TRUST

This word is most often translated *to trust* or *to have confidence in someone*—usually God. But in some contexts it is definitely used to mean hope, as in the great prophetic Twenty-second Psalm. The Messiah's thoughts while suffering on the cross are predicted here: "But thou [God] art he that took me out of the womb: thou didst make me HOPE [*batach*] when I was upon my mother's breasts" (Psalms 22:9 KJV).

Here *batach* is used in the sense of hope that comes from casting one's total future upon God as a little child and trusting Him for everything.

King David also uses this word as he expresses his hope in the resurrection of his body out of death. Joyously he exclaims the following hope, "Therefore my heart is glad, and my glory rejoiceth: my flesh also shall rest in *HOPE*. For thou wilt not leave my soul in hell; neither wilt thou suffer thine Holy One [the Messiah] to see corruption" (Psalms 16:9, 10 KJV).

The basic root idea of confident trust is predominant in the

hope expressed above. David's hope of resurrection was sure because God showed him that the Messiah would be resurrected,
thus guaranteeing the resurrection of all believers.

Abraham is the great example of this particular kind of hope.
In fact, this word was often used in connection with his life. The
New Testament comments on his hope and faith as follows:
"Against all hope, Abraham in *HOPE* believed and so became the
father of many nations . . ." (Romans 4:18 NIV).

Humanly speaking, Abraham wasn't a good candidate as a
daddy. He was about one hundred years old, which is a pretty
advanced age for having children, even in a time of healthy living.
His wife was barren all her life and was pushing ninety. The situation was hopeless from the standpoint of all human logic. Yet God
promised that Abraham and his wife Sarah would have a son
through whom He would raise up a race that would be a blessing
to the whole world. Against the hopeless prospect of what mere
human ability could produce, Abraham hoped in God's promise.
Through this hope he became strong in faith.

The secret of his hope was simply this, "[he was] fully per-
suaded that God had power to do what he had promised"
(Romans 4:21 NIV).

Hope depends upon knowing what the promises of God are,
and also knowing that every promise in the Bible is still personally valid. This was a hang-up for me at first, because I didn't see
how promises made to other people several thousand years ago
were still true for me.

It was then that I began to see verses that clearly indicated
that the personal histories of people in the Bible who believed
or disbelieved God's Word were written to teach *me*. I began
to see the fact that God always kept His promises to those who
hoped and believed in Him, not to those who deserved His favor.

This is made clear in the following, "For whatever was written
in earlier times was written for our instruction, that through perseverance and the encouragement of the Scriptures we might
have HOPE" (Romans 15:4).

And again concerning the continuing validity of God's promises,
"Therefore, let us fear lest, while a promise remains of entering
His rest, any one of you should seem to have come short of it.

For indeed we have had good news preached to us, just as they also; but the word they heard did not profit them, because it was not united by faith in those who heard" (Hebrews 4:1, 2).

I have found that in my life the most treasured asset has been simply to know that God's promises are still valid for me, and that He has the power to do what He has promised.

This persuasion causes a deep settled hope to become the foundation of my life upon which faith can operate in specific daily incidences. Daily faith may waver at times, but if you have grown in your hope in God and His Word, it will operate like an anchor to keep you from drifting during the storms of life.

CHASAH: HOPE THAT GIVES REFUGE

This is a beautiful word for hope. Its root meaning is "to seek shelter, refuge or protection in something or someone." [87]

It is used frequently to portray little animals taking refuge in the cleft of a rock as in Psalms 104:18: ". . . the rocks are a REFUGE for the badgers" (Revised Standard Version, *italics mine*).

Figuratively it came to be used of man's taking refuge in God from the spiritual, emotional, and physical dangers of life. On a few occasions this concept is translated HOPE.

In Proverbs 14:32 this is used in a unique way: "The wicked is driven away in his wickedness: but the righteous hath hope in his death" (KJV). When the one who has been declared righteous by believing in Jesus as his Savior faces death, he will have a hope that is a refuge from the uncertainty and fear presented by his own death.

If ever there's a time that we need a refuge to give us security and confidence it is when either someone we love is dying or when we ourselves are about to die.

The content of this hope is reflected in David's familiar Shepherd's Psalm, "Even though I walk through the valley of the shadow of death, I fear no evil; for Thou art with me . . ." (Psalms 23:4). The Psalmist is referring to that time when we know that we are approaching death. He says that our confidence is that God is with us and will lead us through the dark hours to the brilliant light of His presence on the other side, where we are assured we will live forever. What a hope to take refuge in!

In this generation of accelerating stresses and dangers, we need to learn to focus on the many promises of hope that can shelter our lives from these things.

SABAR: HOPE THAT LOOKS INTENTLY
TO THE PROMISE

This word's root meaning gets at the most basic characteristic of hope: to look intently toward a promise for the future. Its original root meaning is "to inspect, examine, look intently at something." [88]

An Israeli king named Hezekiah who had just been miraculously delivered from death by cancer sang this praise, using the word *hope:*

> For Sheol cannot thank Thee,
> Death cannot praise Thee;
> Those who go down to the pit cannot HOPE for Thy faithfulness.
> It is the living who give thanks to Thee, as I do today . . . .
>   Isaiah 38:18, 19

Hezekiah was living with the terrible fear of his disease when he looked intently at the promise which the Prophet Isaiah gave him of being spared from death. He was allowed to live fifteen more years.

Anyone who has been deathly ill can identify with the comfort God's promises can have in that situation. We can gain stability and strength as we look away from the impossible human circumstances that engulf us and look toward the faithfulness of the Lord to keep His word.

In Psalm 119 which describes the practical blessings of meditating upon and keeping God's Word, the Psalmist says, "I HOPE [*sabar*] for Thy salvation, O LORD, and do Thy commandments" (Psalms 119:166).

The Psalmist shows that hope which looks at the promised blessings motivates and inspires us to keep God's commandments today. This gets at the purifying element of hope which the

Apostle John mentions: "Everyone who has this *HOPE* in him purifies himself, just as he [God] is pure" (1 John 3:3 NIV).

HOPE IS A MANY-SPLENDOURED THING

In this brief study of the various Hebrew words for HOPE, we have seen how hope is a multifaceted and important concept for living. The Bible says the three great words of life today are *faith, hope,* and *love.*

Of course the really big question is, "How do I get a hope like this?"

The Bible is very blunt about the fact that *if you don't have a personal relationship with Jesus the Messiah—who is God's only provision of salvation—you are without true HOPE.* The Bible reminds believers, "Remember that you were at that time separate from Christ, excluded from the commonwealth of Israel, and strangers to the covenants of promise, having NO HOPE and without God in the world" (Ephesians 2:12).

It would be difficult to imagine a more desperate condition than this description of a person without Jesus Christ.

The terms of true hope being born in a person are spelled out clearly:

"For God so loved the world that he gave his one and only Son, that whoever believes in him shall not perish but have everlasting life. For God did not send his Son into the world to condemn the world, but to save the world through him. Whoever believes in him is not condemned, but whoever does not believe stands condemned already because he has not believed in the name of God's one and only Son" . . . . "Whoever puts his faith in the Son has eternal life, but whoever rejects the Son will not see that life, for God's wrath remains on him."

John 3:16, 17, 18, 36 NIV

According to these verses there are only two kinds of people that God sees in the world: Those who believe that Jesus died in their place under the penalty of their sins and have received the pardon that He thereby purchased—and those who do not believe this and must stand judgment for their own sins.

One person has *hope*, because of the certainty of forgiveness, acceptance, and everlasting life. The other person must face condemnation and everlasting conscious separation from God under His wrath against not only his sins, but more for rejecting a free pardon that cost God such a great price.

THE MYSTERY OF A NEW HOPE

When you place faith in Jesus Christ, the immediate results are a mystery—and yet it happens. A new hope springs up within you with the first breath of spiritual life.

The Bible describes this mystery as follows: "To them God has chosen to make known among the Gentiles the glorious riches of this mystery, which is Christ in you, the HOPE of glory" (Colossians 1:27 NIV).

This hope involves the assurance of the promises regarding living with God forever with no more tears or sorrows; no more sickness or pain; ruling with Jesus Christ over God's vast universe; enjoying rewards for faithfulness in this life—and myriads more.

HOW HOPE GROWS

It is possible to be a true Christian and not enjoy the benefits of hope. We must learn to appropriate daily the great power that God makes available to every believer through the Holy Spirit.

The moment that we receive Jesus Christ as our personal Savior, the Spirit of God—who is the third Person of the Divine Trinity, co-equal in power, wisdom, and being with the Father and the Son—comes to take up permanent residency in us. He comes to live within, to strengthen and direct our lives when we depend upon Him and make ourselves available to Him.

We can't live the Christian life in a way that pleases God without a moment-by-moment reliance upon the Holy Spirit to take our human personality and work through it. When we do, the results are electrifying. The Holy Spirit enables us to resist temptations, overcome bad habits, have strength to obey God's commands, understand God's will and His Word.

Yet one of the most important things the Holy Spirit does is to cause hope to grow in us. The Holy Spirit is the *power* behind hope that makes it grow as this verse shows: "May the God of HOPE fill you with great joy and peace as you trust in him, so that you may overflow with HOPE by the power of the Holy Spirit" (Romans 15:13 NIV).

Maybe as you read about these things you have realized that you really don't have this kind of hope because you've never personally invited Jesus Christ to come into your life and thanked Him for purchasing a pardon for your sins. If this is the case, why don't you just pause right now and talk to God in the quiet of your heart. He will hear you because He knows everything in your mind right now. God is anxious to receive you into His family and no one's sins are too great to exceed the value of the pardon that Jesus purchased.

It may be that you are a true believer, but you are discouraged and need to appropriate new hope. If you know of some sin in your life, then confess it to God and thank Him for your forgiveness which is already a settled fact. (*See* 1 John 1:7–2:2.) Then stop trying to live for God by your own human strength and simply ask the Holy Spirit to take over your life. Moment by moment continue to have an attitude of trust in the Holy Spirit to give you an understanding of God's promises and the strength to believe them.

As you do this, the Spirit will cause *HOPE* to overflow in your life and bring you a joy and peace that passes understanding.

I *guarantee* it—God has *promised* it and I've tried it. I've seen that it's true!

I decided a long time ago that it was less difficult to believe that the Bible was what it claimed to be than to disbelieve it.

ABRAHAM LINCOLN

8

The Hope Book

For those of us in the free world it is mind-boggling to realize that almost half of the people on planet earth live in countries where most of their political and civil rights are denied.

When freedom is suppressed, where can people look for hope?

One man who has known both slavery and freedom is the exiled Russian writer and Nobel Prize winner, Aleksandr Solzhenitsyn. He said, "Is it possible to transmit the experience of those who have suffered to those who have yet to suffer? Can one part of humanity learn from the bitter experience of another? Is it possible to warn someone of danger?" [89]

What really becomes important when an individual is suffering? If we were existing under conditions where we were stripped of comforts, denied basic necessities, where would we grope for a source of hope?

A young Soviet Christian knew what it was to suffer. Aida was very frail, but she spent four years in a Russian labor camp for boldly speaking up for her belief in Jesus Christ. When she was asked what was most painful about prison, she didn't talk about the food, the cold, or the loneliness. She said, "It was living without the Gospel that was the most difficult. Having been in prison for some time, I asked for a Bible, but wasn't given one. A sister brought me the Gospel of Mark. When the guards found out I had a Gospel, they were frightened. They searched the camp. Twice they set out on a search for that Gospel, and the second time they found it. For that I was locked up for ten days and ten nights in solitary confinement, in the cold detention cell of prison." [90]

In solitary! For having one book of the Bible!

Aida continued her story, "Although prison conditions were very trying, hope also was with me . . . . For three years I was able to live with the words from Matthew, 'For my yoke is easy and my burden is light.'" [91]

The Bible is the source of hope.

SOMETHING TO DIE FOR

From the first to the twentieth century, Christians have been martyred and imprisoned for believing the Bible. No other book has motivated so many to sacrifice so much.

Among the first evangelists for Jesus Christ were many who died for the truths which Christ taught, which were later recorded in the Scriptures.

Stephen was a deacon of the first Christian church. For his belief he was stoned to death. Peter was crucified with his head down. Andrew was ordered to be crucified and remained tied to a cross for three days before he died. Bartholomew was beaten alive before being beheaded. Thomas was run through with a spear while preaching. Many accounts say that Matthew was beheaded. Mark was seized by a furious mob who was worshiping pagan deities, dragged with a rope around his neck in the streets until his flesh was torn and bloody, and he died.[92]

Before they died, the preaching of the apostles reached into the Roman empire and many believed in Jesus Christ. One bold bishop, Ignatius of Antioch, who heard the gospel from the Apostle John and believed, was cast into prison by the emperor, and after being dreadfully scourged was compelled to hold fire in his hands and endure the agony of having papers dipped in oil put to his sides and lighted.[93]

In France during the 1500s the Oguier family were all burned for their belief in the Bible. When Robert Oguier, the father, was urged to turn from his faith and save himself, he said, "I believe what the holy prophets and apostles have written, and in that faith will I live and die."

When Baudicon Aguier, Robert's son, was dragged to the stake to be burned, he began to sing the Sixteenth Psalm. An onlooker taunted him, "Do you not hear what wicked errors these heretics sing . . . ?"

It must have been through excruciating pain as the flames began to lick around his feet that Baudicon shouted in reply, "How, simple idiot, callest thou the psalms of the prophet David errors?" [93a]

They died for the certain hope based upon the truth of the Bible.

In Spain during the 1600s, a young man named Juliano attempted to take a great number of Bibles concealed in wine casks into his own country. He succeeded in distributing some Bibles, but was betrayed and taken before the Inquisition. Juliano was seized, along with eight hundred persons who had purchased those Bibles! All of them were tortured. Juliano was burned; twenty were roasted on spits; several were imprisoned for life; some were publicly whipped; and many were sent to the galleys.[94]

Their martyrdom was endured because of their certain hope in the promises of the Bible.

In England in the 1500s a man whose name has gone through the centuries as one of God's outstanding servants, William Tyndale, spent a great part of his life translating the Scriptures. His dedication in bringing the Word of God to the common people resulted in his imprisonment and execution. When he was being tied to the stake he cried out, "Lord, open the King of England's eyes!"[95]

Tyndale died because he believed in the certain hope of the Bible's reliability.

In our times people risk their health, their lives, and their earthly possessions to bring the Bible to those without hope. Brother Andrew, the remarkable man who has taken Bibles into countries where God is supposed to be dead, tells the story about a Russian pastor named Ivanhoff. Brother Andrew was not sure he could trust Ivanhoff, because he had told a visiting youth delegation that there was no religious persecution in Russia. Brother Andrew knew this was not true. However, when there was no one around to hear their conversation, Ivanhoff told Brother Andrew he wanted to show him something. He held out his hands and said, "Do you see these nails?"

His fingernails were ridged and thick—the way nails become when they have been torn out by the roots. Ivanhoff continued, "I have spent my time in prison for the faith."[96]

For the hope contained in the Bible, men will undergo torture.

Brother Andrew tells the story about going to China and finding a well-stocked Bible store behind the Bamboo Curtain. He was amazed that such a store could exist, but dismayed when he found out that hardly anyone ever went in. He said, "Strangely enough I left that wide open, well-stocked Bible shop more discouraged than at any time since I had been in China. Persecution is an enemy the Church has met and mastered many times. Indifference could prove to be a far more dangerous foe." [97]

Richard Wurmbrand, who spent fourteen dreadful years in Communist prison camps, has seen modern martyrdom for the truth of the Bible. He wrote, "American Christians swim in Bibles but many don't really know this Holy Book." [98]

MORE THAN POSITIVE THINKING

Could all the men, women, and children throughout the centuries who have been burned, whipped, torn to shreds, starved, and crucified for believing that the Bible contains the truth of God have been sustained if the Bible was a lie?

No one could lay aside tangible comforts and pleasures today if he thought that his hope of future reward in God's presence might be based on a hoax!

I'm sure this is one of the reasons why the Bible makes such strong claims about its credibility as this:

> All Scripture is God-breathed and is useful for teaching, rebuking, correcting, and training in righteousness.
> 2 Timothy 3:16 NIV

Scripture is a technical term for all that's contained in the Bible. The claim of the Scriptures of being God-breathed is unique. It means that the very words were breathed out by God— in the same way He breathed His life and image into man He has breathed His life and image into the Bible.

It is truly a *living* Bible.

CERTAIN HOPE

Our whole basis of having confidence and boldness in living for God comes out of knowing that God's promises have been accurately written and preserved for us. Without this assurance, there can be no certain hope.

Certainty of hope comes from knowing both the trustworthiness of the person who has made the promise, and the reliability of the writings in which those promises are contained.

The supreme goal of the Bible is to reveal to man what God is like and bring us to know and trust Him personally. Isn't it logical that to have a true knowledge of God we must have accurate writings to reveal Him?

In ancient times mirrors were made of polished bronze. Even the best had imperfections so that no one got a really true reflection of himself. Today we have mirrors which show us how we look because they are made of better materials with precision. When God chose to reflect Himself to man, He didn't create an imperfect instrument to do so. The Bible is God's perfect mirror.

God knew that it was imperative that man receive an accurate reflection of His character and personality. Errors in understanding God's character will result in errors of living.

JESUS STAKED ALL ON THE LITERAL OLD TESTAMENT

Jesus testified as he quoted a verse from the Old Testament that it was "the Word of God" and that "the Scripture cannot be broken" (*see* John 10:35).

In this remarkable passage Jesus equates the term *Scripture* with the Word of God and showed that it was a common way of referring to the books of the Old Testament.

Paul said that the Scriptures were "God-breathed." Jesus said that the Scriptures could not be broken—their authority was absolute and unchangeable.

The Apostle Peter, in his last letter which was written about A.D. 66, showed that the Apostle Paul's letters were recognized as Scripture at that time. Peter wrote:

> Bear in mind that our Lord's patience means salvation, just as
> our beloved brother Paul also wrote you with the wisdom that
> God gave him. He writes the same way in all his letters, speaking

in them of these matters. His letters contain some things that are
hard to understand, which ignorant and unstable people distort,
as they do other Scriptures, to their own destruction.

2 Peter 3:15 NIV

In this statement, Peter assumes that Paul's letters were already
widely recognized as Scripture. The book of the Bible, Second
Peter, was a letter addressed to the believers throughout the
world of his day. He made no elaborate explanation about the
assertion concerning Paul, but Peter ascribes the authority of
God's Word to Paul's letters since he states that distorting them
would result in personal destruction.

Today we sometimes use restraint, instead of proclaiming as
boldly as Peter. When people distort what the Bible says, using
it to prove their own convictions, they are "ignorant and unstable"
and only hurt themselves.

A DIVINE-HUMAN CREATION

The most extraordinary and unique claim of the Bible about
itself is that although human beings were used to write it, *the
words are exactly the ones that God wanted to say.*

Peter knew that his death was very near when he wrote his
second letter. Knowing this, he wrote what he considered to be
one of the most important truths that he could leave behind
for us:

Above all, you must understand that no prophecy of Scripture
came about by the prophet's own interpretation. For prophecy
never had its origin in the will of man, but men spoke from God
as they were carried along by the Holy Spirit.

2 Peter 1:20, 21 NIV

These verses declare that the Spirit of God so moved upon the
authors of Scripture that without giving up their own individual-
ity, personality, or personal experiences, God's complete Revelation to man was inerrantly written.

THE WORDS ARE INSPIRED

According to the Bible's own claim, the very words of Scripture were taught the authors by the Spirit of God. Listen to the Apostle Paul as he describes how he and the other writers of Scripture wrote their letters: ". . . which things we also speak, not in words taught by human wisdom, but in those taught by the Spirit, combining spiritual thoughts with spiritual words" (1 Corinthians 2:13).

This is an extremely important claim since there is a school of theologians commonly called the neo-orthodox which teaches that the thoughts of the Bible are divinely inspired, but not the words. Only one who has swallowed the irrational double-talk of Kierkegaardian existentialism could believe such an illogical proposition!

At a recent church convention in Los Angeles the top official of a major denomination said, "Hold fast to the Scriptures as the Word of God, but not as the words of God." [99]

These are common thoughts expressed by so-called liberal churchmen. It isn't surprising that their preaching lacks real life-changing power. They spend more time on political and social issues than on bringing people into a new spiritual birth.

Man cannot think in precise logical terms apart from words. I must add that I made that statement at a meeting one time and was challenged by a woman who had a deaf child. I agree with her that in these cases thinking does occur without words. As she told me, "The problem is in communicating the thoughts without words." She pointed out that accurate thoughts could be conveyed without words through pictures or pantomime.

However, words are conceptual bricks out of which we build the structure of rational thought. We cannot have a Bible filled with erroneous words (as the neo-orthodox theologians teach), and still have accurate thoughts.

We can have feelings or "experiences" without words, as some of the aimless chanting in Eastern religions and certain cults determine, but we certainly cannot have what the Scriptures call a "sound mind."

Jesus and the apostles believed that the Scriptures were infallible right down to the words. In fact, Jesus built some of his most important arguments with the religious experts on the tense of a verb. (*See* Matthew 22:31–33 where Jesus argued for the truth of the resurrection on the basis of the present tense of one verb translated, *I am.*)

Consequently, if Jesus, the apostles, and the Bible itself claim accuracy extending to the words, who has the right to ignore or reject this basic proposition? We have these alternatives: we must reject both the words and the thoughts, or accept them both. There is no honest or rational way to accept one without the other. The Bible never left us that option.

Fortunately, there is ample evidence to accept the accuracy and therefore the authority of the Bible. Thank God for this, for if it were not so, I wouldn't be writing this book. Without the authority of the Bible there would be no sure basis for hope in the world.

Let's look at a short summary of some of the high points of pertinent evidence on the authority of the Bible.

THE MIRACLE OF COMPOSITION

The Bible was written by about forty different authors from various times, cultures, and backgrounds over a period of approximately sixteen hundred years. They were shepherds, judges, kings, farmers, scholars, fishermen, tax collectors, priests, prophets, and doctors.

The marvel is that what they wrote all fits together into a cohesive and homogeneous whole to form one book. It has a consistent view of God, man, redemption, ethics, and morality throughout. It has developed a progression of thought from beginning to end. What is begun as a seed idea at first blossoms into a complete doctrine by the end.

The theologian Dr. Lewis S. Chafer summed up this phenomenon beautifully when he said, "The Bible is not the sort of book that mere men could write, nor would if they could." The more I read the Bible, the more accurate and incisive I see Dr. Chafer's statement to be.

Let's take, for instance, the Bible's concept of man's coming into a relationship with God.

Every other religious book or philosophy teaches that man must in some way do something to earn a right relationship with God; or as in the case of some, that man is a god himself and needs only to be enlightened to what he is.

By contrast, here is what the Bible teaches about God: He is the supreme unique source of all things; He is a personal being and our personality corresponds. to His; He is so holy and pure that man could never earn His acceptance by any system of religious self-effort; in pure undeserved love He has taken upon Himself the punishment due us and died for our rebellion so that He is now righteous and free to forgive totally anyone who believes that God through Jesus Christ has done this for him.

Man could not possibly originate such a plan of salvation! It is completely contrary to our fallen natures which always want to maintain some form of personal merit before God. However, God's plan absolutely rejects human effort and presents salvation as a gracious work of God for man which we can only receive as a gift. Let's face it: we in our fallenness just can't be that objective about ourselves. Man from birth is blinded to the fact that he has no merit acceptable to God. We only learn this and accept it by a divine Revelation.

THE MIRACLE OF PRESERVATION

The Bible is a miracle of survival. No book has been so tenaciously preserved in its original purity in the face of relentless efforts down through history to destroy and discredit it.

We have more manuscript evidence to establish the veracity of every chapter of the New Testament than we have evidence that Aristotle or Julius Caesar ever lived. How few people today are actually aware of this!

F. J. A. Hort spent twenty-eight years studying the New Testament original text. His and Brooke F. Westcott's *Introduction to the New Testament* is called "an achievement never surpassed in the scholarship of any country." Dr. Hort made the following observation after a lifetime of investigation and study: ". . . in the variety and fullness of the evidence on which it rests the text of the New Testament stands absolutely and unapproachably alone among ancient prose writings." [100]

With the great numbers of manuscripts which are from widely separated places and times, careful scientific comparison was made possible. The results have been astounding. Out of the approximately 200,000 words of the New Testament, only about 400 words are in question as to their meaning in the original.[100a] If we never found the original of these few words, no significant understanding of even one doctrine would be changed. These statements were made by great scholars such as Norman L. Geisler, William Nix, and A. T. Robertson, who are widely known to theologians.

The Old Testament has the same reliable evidence. According to Moses, one of the great reasons for the creation of the race of the Jews was so that they could receive, write down, and preserve God's Revelation to man. The nation of Israel accomplished this great service for man with incredible zeal and tenacity.

The chief significance of the Dead Sea Scrolls was that they helped confirm the amazing job of preservation of the Old Testament by the Jewish priests, scribes, and prophets.

Prior to the discovery in 1947 of the complete manuscript of Isaiah contained in the Dead Sea Scrolls, the earliest manuscript we had was from A.D. 900. However, the Dead Sea Isaiah was scientifically dated by Carbon 14 to be at least 200 B.C.—a spread of 1100 years. However—and this is very important—when they were compared word by word, there was virtually no difference.

SO WHAT?

You may be saying to yourself, So what? The reason that I believe it is so necessary to consider a few of these things is because if God has spoken to man in the Bible, it is imperative to have confidence that what we have preserved for us is accurate. In this way hope can be founded upon the certainty of the promises which gave it birth.

WHAT ABOUT THE TRANSLATIONS?

In our modern relative-thinking society, the idea has been set forth that we really can't be sure of any ancient literature written in another language, not only because of alleged loss of the original documents, but also because of loss of meaning in translation.

I have personally translated the New Testament from the original Greek to English, and can testify that several of the modern-day translations are extremely accurate.

I have also worked with many Old Testament passages in the original Hebrew and can attest that nothing essential to knowing God's truth is lost in most translations.

An absolutely astounding fact is that there are more scholarly works available on the grammar, syntax, and word meanings of the original languages of the Bible than there are on modern English or any other modern language. This reflects the sense of importance that has been attached to knowing the Bible's meaning down through history. Scholars have dedicated lifetimes to contribute this wealth of information.

We can be sure that what the Bible promises us is true and reliable under the conditions which have been stated. When we take those promises and mix them with faith, hope has certainty and can raise us out of despair.

This hope can motivate and inspire us to great adventures!

The Bible is the Hope Book.

No wonder the poet David wrote:

> I wait for the LORD, my soul does wait,
> And in His word do I hope.
>> Psalms 130:5

Praise be to the God and Father of our Lord Jesus Christ! In his great mercy he has given us new birth into a living hope . . . .

1 Peter 1:3 NIV
(APOSTLE PETER to
First-Century Believers)

9

Hope Is Born

I once heard about a barge which sank in the New York harbor. It settled in the Hudson River bottom and became deeply embedded. The owners surveyed the mess and wondered what to do about an expensive piece of property stuck in the muck.

Efforts were made to raise and salvage the barge; gigantic floating cranes were brought in, but the mud clung to the vessel and it wouldn't budge. No man-made device had enough power to hoist it out of the mire.

Then a tug-boat captain had an idea. He had deep-sea divers attach cables to the sunken boat. At low tide the ends of the cables were fastened to other boats and all the slack tightened. When the tide began to rise, the power of the Atlantic Ocean began relentlessly to buoy up the various vessels until finally the sunken barge was pulled free of the river bottom and slowly raised to the surface.

Our lives can become as embedded in the muck of depression and despair as that barge. If that happens human efforts are useless. Only the hope inspired by the promises of the Bible—which are backed by the irrepressible strength of God's power—can pull us loose. When we surface and are free, the atmosphere has new motivation, peace, and confidence.

I saw the power of this new hope surge into my own life. Before Jesus came into my life I was very depressed. I wondered if there was a reason for living—if there was a worthwhile purpose in life. I wondered if there was any way to have a sense of personal value or genuine enthusiasm—not just a fake facade.

I began to experience an emotional deliverance that was similar to what David, the great folk-song writer of ancient Israel, describes:

I waited patiently for the Lord;
And He inclined to me, and heard my cry.
He brought me up out of the pit of destruction, out of the miry
    clay;

119

And He set my feet upon a rock making my footsteps firm.
And He put a new song in my mouth, a song of praise to our
    God . . . .

                                                    Psalms 40:1–3

Marvelous things began to take place deep within me as God's
Spirit began to sow the seed of hope in my heart through His
promises. As hope silently grew, its branches began to reach out
and touch every area of my life. I didn't understand what was
happening—all I knew was that I had a thirst for learning the
Bible and that something deep inside my mind was being healed.

In place of fear there was growing confidence. In place of
depression there was a new joy. In place of apathy there was
enthusiasm for life. In place of guilt there was an increased understanding of forgiveness. In place of the feeling that I was worth-
less, there was a sense of self-worth. In place of rejection grew
a knowledge of acceptance.

Why did these changes take place—not just in my life, but in
the lives of so many who believe in and accept Jesus Christ?
Sure, these were "feelings." But the Bible reveals the facts behind
those feelings.

HOPE INSPIRED BY THE NEW BIRTH

Jesus once told a searching theologian the most important
factor in truly understanding God and His Kingdom. He put it
this way: ". . . I tell you the truth, unless a man is born again,
he cannot see [perceive] the kingdom of God" (John 3:3 NIV).

When the religious teacher (whose name was Nicodemus)
heard this amazing statement, he immediately responded, "But
. . . how can a man be born when he is old? Surely he cannot
enter a second time into his mother's womb to be born!" (John
3:4 NIV).

This man was considered the leading teacher in Israel. If de-
grees and honorary doctorates were bestowed, he probably would
have had a long line of credits after his name. However, he didn't
understand how a man could be born again. Nicodemus knew

many facts, but had no spiritual insight. He was brilliant—but spiritually dead.

Jesus continued to clarify exactly what sort of birth He was referring to: "Flesh gives birth to flesh, but the Spirit gives birth to spirit" (John 3:6 NIV).

Jesus explains that a spiritual birth is necessary; man is born physically by the first birth, but he has no spiritual life. *A person must be born again.*

Spiritual life was lost at the beginning when man chose to reject his relationship with God and go his own independent way. That's what happened way back in the Garden of Eden with Adam and Eve.

LIKE CAN ONLY BEGET LIKE

There is a law on this planet of *homogenesis.* It simply means that like can only give birth to its own kind. Once man lost the spiritual dimension of his being, he could only reproduce a physical being, which Jesus calls "the flesh."

For man to receive spiritual life again it has always required a divine intervention of God's Spirit who miraculously imparts new spiritual life to the person who believes in God's provision of forgiveness.

Here is another intriguing example to me of why understanding the original Greek text of the Bible is so helpful. In the original Greek, each time Jesus said, "You must be born" He used the word *anothen* with it. This shouldn't be translated *again,* but rather *from above.* The word is translated in that manner in other places. (In John 3:31 *anothen* is translated *from above.*)

It must be very important when Jesus kept emphasizing that man must have a spiritual birth "from above" through the Spirit of God. It baffles me how some men—even ministers—can claim to be teaching about Jesus without emphasizing the necessity of the new birth. *No one can be a Christian without a spiritual birth.*

Jesus explained that the Spirit's work in giving this birth is like the wind. (*See* John 3:8.) We can see a tree being bent, but we can't see the wind itself; we can feel it on our skin and be pushed by it. The Holy Spirit works the same way—like the wind. We can see the effect of His work on us, but we can't see the Spirit or understand how He works in our human spirit and soul. We can sometimes feel His presence, but we can't see Him.

God tells us how this miraculous birth is obtained: "Yet to all who received him [Jesus], to those who believed in his name, he gave the right to become children of God—children born not of natural descent, nor of human decision or a husband's will, but born of God" (John 1:12, 13 NIV).

I thank my mother and father that they are my natural parents —but I thank God that I am one of His children!

What happens when a person is "born of God"? At least three mighty things occur inside the newborn individual which give him constant direction for a life filled with hope.

BIRTH OF NEW LIFE

The wife of one of my teaching associates recently had a baby. I received an excited call from Tom at 3 A.M. "Hal, we have a little girl—she's gorgeous! It was a completely natural birth—no anesthesia or anything. Naomi feels great and she'll be coming home tomorrow."

Natural birth. This old-new method of childbirth has been gaining attention in medical circles. However, in the true sense this is the manner in which everyone is born.

The Bible calls the life with which we are born soul-life; the original Greek word for this is psuche. The adjective form is psuchikos, which literally means soulish. This is the very word used in 1 Corinthians 2:14 for "natural man" when it says, "But a natural man does not accept the things of the Spirit of God . . . ."

It should read, "A soulish man doesn't accept things of God." The original Greek is so specific—with only a soul, man can't understand divine truth. He must have spiritual life.

Tom and Naomi's baby girl was not born with spiritual life, even though her parents are both Christians. However, as that little girl grows physically she will come to the time when she will need more than the basic physical and material comforts. The need will grow in her heart to know God.

How do we know God when He is not material? God in His very being is spirit; He is not bound by time or space. Jesus said, "God is spirit; and those who worship Him must worship in spirit and truth" (John 4:24).

However, without that spiritual dimension of life, which alone understands the things of God, we don't have the capacity to worship God. The Bible tells us that ". . . a natural man does not accept the things of the Spirit of God; for they are foolishness to him, and he cannot understand them, because they are spiritually appraised" (1 Corinthians 2:14).

The *natural man* or the *natural woman* or *child* is an accurate description of the person who hasn't been born again. Someone in his natural physical state doesn't accept divine phenomena.

A person may be brilliant and successful in business, education, or a profession; he may be a member of a church or synagogue, and still be blind to spiritual truth. The issue is not IQ or basic goodness. The youngest child or the most uneducated person who is born spiritually can understand more about the Bible's true meaning than the most intelligent person who is only a "soulish man."

I was confronted one time by a grad student at one of the leading American universities. In no uncertain terms he made it clear to me that he thought the Bible was stupid. He became quite hostile as he scoffed at biblical miracles.

"Look," he said sarcastically, "how could the Red Sea open up and allow people to pass through? And don't you think it's pretty ridiculous to believe that a man could be swallowed by a giant fish and come out alive three days later? How can you logically explain to me a man walking on the water?"

He looked at me and shook his head, "It's all a bunch of bunk."

I simply told him that the God I had come to know personally can do all these things and more. "Your problem," I said, "is that you have never met the Author of this book—because if you knew Him, you'd know that these are just the sort of things He does."

He was intellectually honest enough not to walk away but to hear me out. "If there is a God," I continued, "then miracles are no problem. But if your only standard of measuring phenomena is human capability then you're in a hopeless position to explain the origin of the universe which is staring you in the face."

Incidentally, this man was born spiritually some time later and then had no problem accepting miracles.

When we are born spiritually we are given a new human spirit. The human spirit which becomes a part of us should not be confused with the Holy Spirit. It is the Holy Spirit, His intelligence, His wisdom, His discernment, which gives our human spirit these attributes and teaches us divine thoughts.

What an amazing concept to grasp! "The Spirit Himself bears witness with our spirit that we are children of God" (Romans 8:16).

No prosecuting attorney could withstand the impact of a witness like that. As the Holy Spirit testifies with our human spirit, we have a case which will win against any attack.

This new life—this new spirit which is a part of our basic being—has the capacity for receiving the Holy Spirit's teaching. It has been promised us:

> But you have an anointing from the Holy One, and you all know . . . . And as for you, the anointing which you received from Him abides in you, and you have no need for any one to teach you; but as His anointing teaches you about all things, and is true and is not a lie, and just as it has taught you, you abide in Him.
>
> 1 John 2:20, 27

The anointing which is spoken of in these verses is the Holy Spirit's teaching ministry. He has come to dwell within us, teaching us through our human spirit to understand spiritual truths.

With the new birth comes this powerful new life—a life of spiritual understanding which grows as we allow the Holy Spirit to teach us through the Bible, prayer, and other believers.

New life—and certain hope. How closely these are related! The new life gives us the capacity to know God, which results in our certain hope because He keeps His promises. The new life gives us the ability to understand the spiritual truths of the Bible and therefore know the ground of our hope.

The new life is the soil in which hope takes root and springs up into our lives, giving us a growing knowledge of our eternal destiny.

BIRTH OF THE NEW NATURE

The auditorium was filled one evening as I spoke to a group of students. Although it's gratifying to have a large audience, many of the most rewarding moments come after the meeting is over. When one young man approached me I remember that he had a look which indicated he had questions—but was a little uncertain what to say.

He told me that he wanted to know about new life in Jesus Christ, but, he said, "I'm just too young—I know myself, I have too many weaknesses and I know how strongly temptation pulls on me. I just couldn't hold out."

I knew what he meant. "Look," I said, "God doesn't want you to make a list of the ten things you love and give them up, and then make a list of ten things you hate and do them. He simply wants you to receive His Son and let Him come into your life and change it. Then God puts this new nature within you—it's this new nature which gives you the new desires. Believe me, your new nature will hold out, because it never stops wanting to follow God."

He looked intently at me, the apprehension beginning to leave him. "Okay," he said quietly, "if God can put something in me that will always want to follow Him no matter what, then I'd like to have it."

So we prayed together and he received Christ right there. A miracle took place. He received a new nature, just as we all do when we are born again.

The Bible explains the principle this way: "No one who is born of God practices sin, because His seed abides in him; and he cannot sin, because he is born of God" (1 John 3:9).

This passage baffles many people. We know that it doesn't mean, as a few teach, that a Christian can't sin. We are told that we're liars if we say we have no sin. (*See* 1 John 1:8, 10.) Does that mean that John is contradicting himself? Not at all.

What it does mean is that the new nature (called *His seed*) which lives in us cannot sin. This nature is born with a whole new set of desires—it always wants to follow God.

Here is where the Christian finds conflict. We have a new nature, given to us at the new birth. But right alongside of this great gift is that unreformable, sinful old nature. We find ourselves caught with this inner storm. Since the old nature cannot be reformed, the more a Christian grows in his spiritual life, the more he is aware of the sharp contrast between the old and the new natures.

It's always reassuring to me that the great Apostle Paul had this same turmoil in his own experience.

Can you feel the anguish of Paul—and put yourself right in the picture—when he says:

> My own behaviour baffles me. For I find myself doing what I really loathe but not doing what I really want to do. Yet surely if I do things that I really don't want to do, I am admitting that I really agree that the Law is good. But it cannot be said that "I" am doing them at all—it must be sin that has made its home in my nature. 'And, indeed, I know from experience that the carnal side of my being can scarcely be called the home of good!' I often find that I have the will to do good, but not the power. That is, I don't accomplish the good I set out to do, and the evil I don't really want to do I find I am always doing. Yet if I do things that I don't really want to do then it is not, I repeat, "I" who do them, but the sin which has made its home within me.
>
> Romans 7:15–20 PHILLIPS

The new nature knows what is right and cannot sin. The old nature knows what is wrong and wants to do it. The believer has a choice: He can give in to the old nature and be dominated by feelings of despair as the habits and attitudes of his old self dominate him; or he can trust the Holy Spirit to empower him to follow the desires of the new nature and know what positive living is all about.

We behave the way we see ourselves. God wants us to accept the new person He has created within us. He wants us to count true the statement in Ephesians which says, "[I am created right now] in the likeness of God . . . in righteousness and holiness of the truth" (Ephesians 4:24).

We find it hard to believe. We say, "Look, my track record is so full of sin and failure that I don't see how I could be holy or blameless." Remember what Paul found was true of himself? He said, "So now no longer am I the one doing the sinning, but the sin which indwells me." (*See* Romans 7:11.)

Paul isolated the source of sin from his real self, which was born of God and holy, and identified it as the old self with its sinful nature which has already been judged. Then he was able to see that he really was a new person, in spite of his failure. He realized that there was no necessity to follow the lusts of the old nature, which God had already judged and forgiven him for its continuing presence.

You may be saying, Okay, that's Paul, not me! It's true, what is part of your old sin nature may not be a part of mine.

One person has a spiteful and gossiping tongue; another explodes with a nasty temper. A woman may grapple with her feelings of jealousy, a man with a craving for alcohol—or another guy's wife.

Sometimes a new believer is changed dramatically when he is born again. But after a time he begins to fall back into the old habits, respond to the former evil he thought he left behind. He finds, like Paul, that he's doing what he doesn't want to do, and even more—he may find he's enjoying his old nature.

Every Christian at some time or another finds himself in the midst of this conflict, but no Christian needs to be defeated.

TONY WAS A NEW MAN

I think one of the clearest illustrations of the conflict between the old and new nature was a friend of mine who had a miraculous deliverance from drugs. But he began to slip. After he had been a Christian for a while he began to go back to the old crowd and their pot parties. He felt the pull of desires from his former life and got into drugs again.

He came to me and said, "Hal, I don't know what's happening

to me—it just seems like the old ways are coming back and I can't shake the habit of pot."

I told him about Romans 6:6 where it says that the old self has been judged in order that we are no longer slaves to our sinful habits. I said, "Tony, God has already judged the old person that you were. You've still got this old nature within you which wants to draw you off into sin, but God has judged that nature and forgiven you for it. Its power over you has been broken!"

As he listened to me I saw the hope growing in him. I told him he could follow the old nature if he chose to, but he could also choose to reject it and then the Holy Spirit would put it down.

Tony looked surprised when I told him he didn't have to follow his old nature any more. God had judged it; He's already forgiven him for it—and as far as God is concerned it doesn't have any right to control him. "The minute you count that true, Tony, the Holy Spirit will back up that step of faith. He will not only overcome the power of that old nature in you as you continue to choose not to follow it, but He will cause you to have strength to follow the desires of the new nature."

He took me at my word. He left with an excited look on his face and when I saw him about a week later he said, "That did it! The old nature's really put down. I just said that I didn't have to smoke pot any more—the real me wants to follow God—and I asked the Lord to back me up."

Tony didn't need theological jargon; he knew the basic principles.

I don't care what your habit is, if you see the miracle that God has performed—that He has so judged your old nature that it has no rights over you, and He has given you a new nature which desires to follow Him—and the Holy Spirit the power to back up this new nature—then you can be delivered from whatever habit you may have.

CATHY WAS A NEW WOMAN

I once knew a girl who became a Christian as a lesbian. We told her that God accepted lesbians and He didn't count her sins any greater than any other sins. She began to experience the wonders of God's acceptance and forgiveness, as she began to grow in His love. However, we made sure that she understood that although God accepted *her*, He didn't accept her behavior.

Cathy had a pattern of thinking which was very difficult to break. However, I told her that her sins had been judged by God and as she chose to believe that her old nature no longer had any right to rule in her life, the Holy Spirit would deliver her from its power.

As Cathy chose to believe that God had broken the power of her homosexual nature, and as she chose to depend upon the Holy Spirit to deliver her from it, she experienced the first deliverance she had ever known.

Cathy was a new—true—woman.

Now you may be saying, "Wait a minute—I don't have anything that drastic to cope with."

I have used extreme examples to show how powerful the apparatus which God has set up inside of you really is. The new forces of life and the power of His Spirit are revolutionary. There are few things which have as strong a grip on people as drug addiction and homosexuality. If God can break those, He can break your habits, whatever they are.

BIRTH OF NEW SELF

There are many books written, many courses given on self-image. Many of them are very helpful, but most of them leave out the greatest source of a new self-image, and that is the new spiritual birth.

Dr. Maxwell Maltz wrote a popular book called *Psycho-Cybernetics*, which is a practical study in self-image psychology. It's interesting that Dr. Maltz didn't start out as a psychologist but a plastic surgeon. However, many cases showed him the truth of the fact that each person has an image of himself deep in his mind, and that he cannot act consistently different from the way he conceives himself to be.

Dr. Maltz writes: "A human being always acts and feels and performs in accordance with what he imagines to be true about himself." [101]

He tells of many cases where the skill of plastic surgery changed the attitude and outlook of his patients. On the other hand, he also told about others who acquired new faces but went right on wearing the old personality.

I remember hearing about the young woman who went to a plastic surgeon with the request for a "nose job." She found it difficult to look at the doctor; she spoke with embarrassment. She came from a family of very attractive people and it was obvious that she felt like the ugly duckling because of her prominent nose.

Plastic surgery was performed on her, the operation was very successful. When the moment of truth came for the bandages to be removed the doctor was amazed by how beautiful the girl was.

He held the mirror up to her face and watched her eyes as she stared at herself. Suddenly she burst into tears. She said, "You see, it didn't work. I look just the same as I did!"

The doctor told her to look again, but she turned her face away from the mirror. She couldn't see her new beauty. She had a self-image of being ugly and even though the facts told her that she was changed, she couldn't alter the way she felt about herself. It was only after six months of consultation with a psychologist that she looked in the mirror and believed what she saw—that she was different.

Her personality then changed almost overnight. She became a warm, outgoing person. She behaved in accordance with what she believed herself to be. She appropriated what she was.

Your self-image reflects the way you act. How you feel about yourself determines how you live.

The most profound changes take place the moment we are born into the new life with Jesus Christ. No plastic surgeon could ever equal His ability to change us. We become new persons—we acquire new self-images.

We are told: "Therefore if any man is in Christ, he is a new creature; the old things passed away; behold, new things have come" (2 Corinthians 5:17).

This verse doesn't say, "He *will* be a new creature." It says, "He *is* a new creature."

As a young believer I had a barrel of bad habits—the grip of my old life was tenacious. I wondered how in the world I could be a new creature. What I failed to see is that in God's dealing with me, He had created a whole new person. I had new life, a new nature, and a new image.

Many of us indulge ourselves in the *if only* philosophy: *if only* I were better looking—*if only* I were thinner—*if only* I had a better education—*if only* I hadn't married him (or her)—*if only* I had a better job.

God didn't give us an *if only* life. He tells us we are new persons. When we begin to see all the things God says He's done for us we begin to get a new image. As our basic self-image changes to what is really true, we begin to behave that way. This is exactly what the surgeon-psychologist, Dr. Maltz, said: We act the way we see ourselves.

Paul explained this to the Ephesians: ". . . that, in reference to your former manner of life, you lay aside the old self, which is being corrupted in accordance with the lusts of deceit, and that you be renewed in the spirit of your mind, and put on the new self, which in the likeness of God has been created in righteousness and holiness of the truth" (Ephesians 4:22–24).

How do you lay aside the old self? By simply believing that God said you don't *have* to be the person you used to be—you don't *have* to obey the old self. How do you put on the new self? As your mind is renewed from reading the Scriptures and asking the Holy Spirit to teach your new spiritual nature, you discover what God says is really true.

You are a new creation.
You are in the likeness of God.
You have been created in righteousness and holiness of truth.

Imagine what it would be like to have someone's cast-off clothes, unwashed and baggy—to have matted hair and dirty skin. Would you enjoy looking at yourself in a mirror? The image would repulse you as much as it did the person who stepped off the sidewalk to avoid getting near you.

Then suppose someone walked over, put an arm around you and said, "Come on, I'm going to take you home, give you a nice room and bath of your own, a good dinner, and some new clothes." After you accept this miraculous invitation, soak in mounds of perfumed suds, dress in the best fashion in tailor-made clothes, and have a delectable dinner, would you look like the same person in the mirror? The image reflected would be a whole new you.

God has given us His best. There is nothing we have done to earn it or deserve it, but we are no longer spiritual bums.

As we believe this our lives will begin to change. In the Christian life, producing true and lasting changes is a matter of becoming what we already are. It's a matter of believing what God has already made us.

As the field of psychology has discovered, it's impossible for a person to make lasting changes in his life until his image of himself has changed. I'm sure this is why God spends so much time in the Bible telling us what He's already done for us.

New life. New nature. New image. As we think about these three mighty things which take place in this new spiritual birth, we can understand why this is the birth of hope. We have the foundation for a whole new life. We have the potential for living the life which is pleasing to God.

When we are pleasing Him, we are enjoying ourselves. When we like ourselves, we relate better to others and they respond more positively to us.

And that's power for positive hope.

But by the grace of God I am what I am . . . .
1 Corinthians 15:10

10

Verdict: Not Guilty

God forgives you. God accepts you. What an impact those two concepts can have on a person's life! Hope lives when forgiveness and acceptance are the daily nutrition. Hope becomes sick and undernourished when those vital growth elements are forgotten or misunderstood.

A woman I never met wrote me a letter which gave a dramatic example of how understanding God's forgiveness and acceptance can change the direction of a life.

The woman was obviously educated and articulate; she told me of her background—how she had been raised in a good home, attended church all her life, and had come to believe in Jesus Christ at an early age. She was on many church committees and considered herself someone who had an acceptable spiritual life. Her husband held a responsible position, they had two lovely children who were in their teens, a beautiful home, and were respected in the community.

Everything was going very well until she had an affair and committed adultery. It was then that the inadequacy of her spiritual understanding became evident in her life. Immediately she began to think there was no more forgiveness for her—she believed that God had rejected her. She went into her room and sobbed her confession of sin, but she didn't feel as if her prayers were reaching God.

The pressure built up inside of her so that she finally thought of taking her life. She began to plot her death, planning it carefully, so that it would look accidental and not bring shame to her family.

She set the time for the suicide. The day before the fatal date someone gave her a copy of *Satan Is Alive and Well on Planet Earth*. She had no idea of reading the book, but as she thumbed through her eyes stopped on the chapter on guilt. She began to read and gradually she saw things she had never understood. She

135

kept thinking to herself, *If only it could really be true*—that *God still loves and accepts us even after we willfully sin.*

As she read about the fact that what Jesus did at the cross was sufficient to pay for our sins past, present, and future, she began to think, *If only this is really true.*

She decided to try one more time to confess her sin. She said, "Lord, I'm going to take You at Your word and believe that You have really forgiven me."

This time it was different. A tremendous weight seemed to be taken from her and she immediately felt a rush of hope, knowing that she really was God's child.

She got up from her knees and said she felt new all over—she had a purpose for living. For days she was deliriously happy, and began to tell others about the forgiveness and acceptance that there is in Jesus Christ.

She closed her letter by saying:

I wonder how many others there are like me who are deprived for so long of knowing about God's acceptance and forgiveness? I wonder why I never learned that there's no sin too great if we'll just turn to God and confess it and start trusting Him again.

I raised this question myself. "I wonder how many people there are who are lost in the depression and ultimate despair of not knowing they're forgiven?"

In twenty years of counseling and from the experiences in my own life, I believe that the source of the greatest problems which we bear are carrying unnecessary guilt on our shoulders and being oppressed by false guilt.

LEGAL GUILT

There are basically three things we need to know about the subject of guilt.

First, there is *legal guilt*. When we sin and break God's law we are legally guilty and must be judged and punished. It's this guilt that Jesus Christ took upon Himself at the cross and bore judgment in our place. He died under the penalty of that guilt.

In the New Testament there's a beautiful word that is little understood—*propitiation*. This word encompasses the whole concept of Christ's being judged in our place in order that God can be free to love and accept us. The best short definition of that word is that "God isn't angry at us any more," because He's taken His anger out on Jesus Christ and all of the just payment for the penalty of our legal guilt was poured out on Him.

When we believe in Jesus Christ as our Savior, the legal guilt is taken away forever. This is why the Scripture says, "There is therefore now no condemnation for those who are in Christ Jesus" (Romans 8:1).

The Bible teaches that one who believes in Jesus Christ is not punished by God—but disciplined. These are two different procedures. Punishment involves inflicting penalty for an offense; it deals with the legal consequences of sin. Punishment focuses on past misdeeds and is inflicted in righteous anger. The result in the person who is being punished is fear, guilt, hostility, and despair.

But since Jesus Christ took our punishment God isn't angry with us any more. (There's that word: *propitiation*.) Because of what Christ has done for us, God can forgive our sins.

Discipline, on the other hand, is to correct us and encourage positive growth. It doesn't focus on the past, but always toward the future.

The attitude that God has in disciplining is love. Hebrews 12:5–11 says that "Whom the Lord loves He disciplines and chastens."

The resulting emotion in the one He disciplines is that of security; it's knowing that He really cares and is looking out for our best interests.

In our relationships with our children, as Dr. James Dobson points out in his book *Dare to Discipline*, "Children thrive best in an atmosphere of genuine love, undergirded by reasonable, consistent discipline."

As God's children, we thrive best under His loving discipline. This doesn't mean that all discipline is particularly pleasant—a child of any age knows that. But from discipline we grow; we become strong and secure human beings, able to cope with the challenges of life.

NEUROTIC GUILT

Another aspect of guilt is sometimes tagged as a *guilt complex* or *neurotic guilt*. This is a false guilt and is one of the most destructive forces in a person's life. God is *not* the source of this kind of guilt.

The erosion of neurotic guilt begins when we commit either a real or an imagined sin and fail to believe in or claim God's forgiveness.

Imagined sins are the things we have come to believe are wrong through the effect of our culture, parents, friends, and false religious teaching. Sometimes we believe we are sinning and feel guilty over something that the Bible never labeled as sin.

Then there is the graduated scale of sins. In our minds we categorize them from "X-rated" to "G-rated." There are the vile and filthy sins all the way down to the sins fit for general audience consumption. We feel extremely guilty if we commit a horrible sin like adultery, but not very guilty at all if we gossip and malign someone's character.

The problem with this kind of thinking is that God doesn't have a graduated sin scale. In the eyes of God it's just as bad to be angry as to murder. (*See* Matthew 5:21, 22.)

We need to look at sin from God's perspective—not man's.

Real sin is actually labeled by God's Word as wrong. When we know that we have committed real sin, then we need to immediately remember and believe that Jesus Christ has already been punished in our place for the *legal guilt* of it. Because of this God will not reject us as His children; He will not deal with us in anger; He will not punish us to get even for what we have done, but rather will discipline us for our good.

In the following Scriptures God assures us of this:

My dear children, I write this to you so that you will not sin. But if anybody does sin, we have one who speaks to the Father in our defense—Jesus Christ, the Righteous One. He is the atoning sacrifice for our sins, and not only for ours but also for the sins of the whole world.

1 John 2:1, 2 NIV

Some people look upon Christians as belonging to some sort of a spiritual elite—members of a club with secret rites and passwords. Christians may have an *inclusive* club, but it is not restricted. In the above passage, and many more, are the rights of free entry which tell us that Jesus Christ has satisfied God's righteous demands not only for the believers, but also for the whole world.

Jesus is our constant defender when we sin as Christians. He has perfect grounds for our defense—He has already paid for every one of our offenses, therefore He never loses a case.

It's important to understand that Jesus doesn't have to defend us against God the Father, but rather against the accusations which Satan brings before the Father. (*See* Revelation 12:10.)

Satan says, "Take a look at that smug Christian. What makes him think he's so good when he cheated on his income tax five years ago?"

Jesus immediately steps in as our Defense Attorney and pleads His atoning death as full payment for our sins. Then the Father declares, "Case dismissed!" and throws Satan out of court.

If we need a lawyer to defend us against a serious charge, we would search for the best one we could get. Whenever we follow a prominent case in the newspapers, we read the questions of the reporters to the attorneys, and try to follow the skill with which the defense and the prosecution make their points.

However, a lawyer could leave his client—either of his own free will or because he suddenly had a heart attack or was hit by a car.

On the other hand, the Scriptures say that Jesus Christ is always on hand to intercede on our behalf, "but He, on the other hand, because He abides forever, holds His priesthood permanently. Hence also He is able to save forever those who draw near to God through Him, since He always lives to make intercession for them" (Hebrews 7:24, 25).

We can't lose. Of course we sin as believers, but He constantly pleads His death on our behalf as full legal payment for sins.

The only way one of us who has been born into God's family can be lost would be for Jesus to die. However, He lives forever and He saves forever.

When we believe these facts and honestly confess our sins to

God, neurotic guilt is blasted loose from our troubled minds. However, we must clearly understand that a sense of forgiveness doesn't come from a hollow confession. We must believe in the sufficiency of Christ's death in our place as the perpetual ground of our forgiveness.

Believing these truths doesn't give us a license to sin, but to serve. The Holy Spirit faithfully works along with our new nature to make us desire to serve the Lord. But neurotic guilt can cause us to think that repentance and confession are hopeless unless we apply these truths I'm talking about.

If we try to play games with God, then in love He will correct the error of our ways and bring us back.

This never-ending forgiveness is promised in God's great letter to the Hebrew believers, written in the first century. It is just as true in the twentieth century. These Jews were still confused about the relationship of Christ's sacrifice to the animal sacrifices of the Law of Moses. The Bible says, "By this will we have been sanctified through the offering of the body of Jesus Christ once for all . . . . For by one offering He has perfected for all time those who are [being] sanctified" (Hebrews 10:10, 14).

An Israeli friend of ours, raised in the orthodox tradition of animal sacrifices, came to believe in Jesus Christ when she realized that He was the "once for all" sacrifice.

SANCTIFICATION: ETERNAL AND DAILY

Sometimes we hear terms being used which at first don't seem particularly relevant to our everyday challenges of family, job, and friends. But they are basic. *Sanctification* is one of those basic terms.

In the Bible sanctification means to set something apart to God. There are four kinds of sanctifications and two of them are found in the verses from Hebrews 10. The first, in verse 10, refers to the eternal unchangeable sanctification at salvation. God sets us apart as His eternal possession.

The second sanctification found in Hebrews 10:14 refers to a daily process whereby the Holy Spirit progressively sets apart to

God the life of the Christian. It's that wonderful maturing experience that we all go through at varying rates of speed.

Our Israeli friend describes her understanding of God when she says, "Slowly, slowly I began to learn that the God of the Old Testament and God of the New Testament are the same."

If this Hebrew believer, or any other believer, did not understand what the following verse means, the wonderful promise of the one time, perfect sacrifice of Jesus Christ, and all the human blessing surrounding that sacrifice, would be snatched away. Hebrews 10:26 says: "For if we go on sinning willfully after receiving the knowledge of the truth, there no longer remains a sacrifice for sins."

The first thing to know in understanding this verse is for whom was this written and what was their problem?

This letter was written to Hebrew people who had recently come out of a lifetime of being steeped in Judaism, some of which was true and some false.

The problem, which the author of the Book of Hebrews confronts all the way through, is that they were trying to follow Christ and still cling to their Judaism. The most serious aspect of this error was in the area of animal sacrifice versus the sacrifice of Messiah Jesus.

The whole point of Hebrews 10 is that the sacrifice of Jesus for sin did away with the animal-sacrifice system. Therefore, when it says, ". . . there no longer remains a sacrifice for sins," it is referring to the animal sacrifices on which they had depended.

The Hebrew people for whom this was written had been thoroughly exposed to the message about the total sufficiency of Jesus the Messiah's sacrifice. If they rejected this vital truth, then there was no longer any animal sacrifice to fall back on. There were some Hebrews who were not truly believers, so the writer sternly warns them here.

About a year after this letter was written the historic problem ceased to be. The Roman legions of Titus destroyed the Temple at Jerusalem and made it impossible to offer animal sacrifices according to the Judaistic system.

What does this mean to us today? Perhaps we have never had any connection with animal sacrifice, real or symbolic. All of this may seem academic theological nit-picking, and not relevant to a personal belief or spiritual need. The application to us is that if we try to add any form of human merit to the finished atoning work of Christ we nullify its worth and can't become true believers.

I'm aware that a number of ministers teach that Hebrews 10:26 means that if you persist in willful sin there comes a point when you go beyond the sacrifice of Jesus and become lost. If that were true, then there is a diametric contradiction between verse 26 and verses 10, 14, and 17 of Hebrews 10.

Why do I make such a point of this? It's because I've found many believers who truly want to turn from their sins and follow God, but are paralyzed with fear and despair. The woman I mentioned at the beginning of this chapter quoted this exact verse (Hebrews 10:26) as the basis of why she felt she was lost—without hope of forgiveness. This woman missed committing suicide by one day.

Satan is a master of using Scriptures falsely applied to accuse the minds of troubled believers and drive them from the certain hope of continuing forgiveness into neurotic guilt. When this happens there is no way we can trust God so that we can appropriate the power of the Holy Spirit to help us turn from our sins and begin to walk with Him again.

Don't let Satan neutralize your hope and faith with neurotic guilt.

One of the clearest explanations of how to deal with guilt is in the book *Guilt and Freedom* by Bruce Narramore and Bill Counts.[101a]

THE CONVICTION OF THE SPIRIT

Sometimes the conviction that is brought upon a sinning believer is falsely labeled guilt. When we sin as a believer, God the Holy Spirit (who lives within all believers) will faithfully begin to convict us that we are wrong. He will lead us toward turning from the sin to confessing it to God and believing we are forgiven. In other words, the Spirit's conviction produces true repentance.

There is an excellent contrast between what the Spirit's conviction produces and what neurotic guilt produces in 2 Corinthians 7:8–13. In this chapter God shows that the Spirit produces a godly sorrow over sin which leads to true repentance. But neurotic guilt results in what is called ". . . the sorrow of the world [which] produces death" (2 Corinthians 7:10).

These two kinds of sorrow and their results are clearly illustrated in the cases of Judas Iscariot and Peter the Apostle.

Both of these men betrayed Jesus Christ. Judas Iscariot betrayed Jesus by selling Him out to His enemies which led to His arrest and execution. (See Matthew 26:14–16; 47–50.)

Peter betrayed Jesus by denying three times that he even knew Him. In the third denial Mark says of Peter, "He began to call down curses on himself, and he swore to them, 'I don't know this man you're talking about'" (Mark 14:71 NIV). This was an utter denial of Jesus with a solemn oath.

Judas felt sorrow for what he had done when he saw that Jesus was condemned to crucifixion. He even confessed his sin. "'I have sinned,' he said, 'for I have betrayed innocent blood'" (Matthew 27:4 NIV).

He made restitution for his sin: "So Judas threw the money into the temple and left . . ." (Matthew 27:5 NIV). He also wept greatly in regret for what he had done, but he went out and hanged himself.

Peter felt sorrow also and wept bitterly over his great sin of denying Jesus in His darkest hour. (See Mark 14:72.) But Peter went on to become a great apostle.

Why did Judas's life end in such disaster and Peter's with great honor and fulfillment? Was one's sin worse than the other? Certainly not.

Judas never came to believe in his own need for God's provision of forgiveness. Therefore, he never did see that the death of Jesus Christ was sufficient to pardon even his sin if he would have just received it by faith. Unresolved, neurotic guilt took hold of him. It produced regret and sorrow for what he had done, but since he didn't have the hope of God's gift of forgiveness, he quickly fell into despair.

When a man is seized by this everything begins to appear hopeless. At the earliest age we learn that wrongdoing deserves punishment. So since Judas couldn't believe that Jesus was punished for his sin, he hanged himself in utter hopelessness.

Peter, on the other hand, had a godly sorrow which didn't drive him into neurotic guilt, but rather into confession of his sin and claiming of God's forgiveness which was already true for him. Jesus Himself restored Peter to fellowship when He asked him three times, "Simon, do you love Me?" (See John 21:15–19.)

In this incident He recommissioned Peter to go on in the ministry to which He had called him. Peter had returned to Galilee to go back to fishing as a profession, apparently thinking that after such a horrible failure God could never use him again.

So after each question to Peter, the Lord said, "Feed my lambs," "Take care of my sheep," and "Feed my sheep." (See John 21:15, 16, 17 NIV.)

In this wonderful incident the Lord Jesus showed Peter that sin can not only be forgiven, but that God continues to accept us fully and doesn't hold our past sins against us. Jesus showed Peter that he was still called as an apostle. As David puts it so beautifully in the Psalms, "If You, Lord, should keep account of our iniquities, O Lord, who could stand? But there is forgiveness with You, so that You may be reverently trusted." (See Psalms 130:3, 4 amplified from the Hebrew.)

If God kept account of our sins and held them against us, I certainly wouldn't still be in the ministry. And I'm sure that every honest Christian would have to confess the same thing.

What was the secret behind Peter's life that kept him from despair and self-destruction like Judas? The difference was this: Peter had a basic hope inspired by his faith in God's salvation through the Messiah Jesus; even though he had a temporary lapse of operational faith, he didn't plunge below the line of despair where there is no hope.

Peter's hope of forgiveness wasn't clear, but because of his hope inspired by the new nature and the promises of eternal life, he didn't fall into self-destruction as Judas did. In the whole experience, though, Peter learned a much greater lesson. He learned that God's forgiveness through the cross extends to our future sins as well. He learned that the issue in continuing to be used by God is not whether there is enough forgiveness to cover our failure, but whether we will claim the forgiveness that is already an established fact.

What marvelous hope we have in this knowledge of forgiveness to undergird our lives as Christians! As long as we are still breathing God has a purpose for our lives. If you have been thinking that the Lord is finished with you—maybe you've committed some sins that are plaguing you with paralyzing guilt—then listen to me! God has a purpose for you. You can still serve Him.

Jesus said, "I WILL NEVER DESERT YOU, NOR WILL I EVER FORSAKE YOU" (Hebrews 13:5). The issue is whether you believe in the promise of God, "If we confess our sins, He is faithful and righteous to forgive us our sins and to cleanse us from all unrighteousness" (1 John 1:9).

ETERNAL SALVATION? OF COURSE

As far as our eternal salvation is concerned, that is secured once and for all when we believe in Christ as Savior. But as we walk in the Christian life, there is a daily need for cleansing of sin. But be careful of this in your thinking. God doesn't have to forgive you again when you confess sins as a believer. You have already been forgiven legally for every sin you'll commit, past, present, and future. We must, however, appropriate this cleansing and forgiveness to be able to walk in close communion with the Lord and to claim the power of the Holy Spirit for an obedient life.

Sin doesn't cause the Christian to be lost, but it does interrupt fellowship with the Lord and the empowering ministry of the Holy Spirit who lives within.

As Peter learned, his sin didn't cause the Lord Jesus to stop loving him. It didn't cause Him to stop accepting Peter, nor to reject him for service. (Few of us will commit a sin quite as offensive to God as Peter did, however.) After Jesus' Resurrection He sought Peter out and graciously led him back from his defeated sense of rejection and sent him forth with fresh new abounding hope.

As a result Peter learned a lesson that made him able to be the great apostle he became. Before this incident broke him of his pride and self-sufficiency, he was not prepared to wholly depend upon Christ for his strength. But when he was restored with the hope inspired by understanding God's grace, he was no longer self-confident but Christ-confident. Peter became the bold unstoppable apostle that we see blazing a trail of glory across the pages of the Book of Acts.

Peter expresses the deep abiding hope that sustained and motivated his life in one of his letters written late in his life. "Praise be to the God and Father of our Lord Jesus Christ! In his great mercy he has given us new birth into a living hope through the resurrection of Jesus Christ from the dead, and into an inheritance that can never perish, spoil or fade—kept in heaven for you. Through faith you are shielded by God's power until the coming of the salvation that is ready to be revealed in the last time" (1 Peter 1:3–5 NIV).

It was this "living hope" that gave him the joy and courage throughout his life that was filled with hardships, dangers, and constant challenges.

Do you have a *living hope?* Lay hold of the promises of God's forgiveness and acceptance of you. This will bring a hope that will secure you from lapsing into an unproductive, unmotivated Christian life.

There is no reason for a believer to be in defeat and despair, no matter what the circumstances. As Peter said, we have a hope of an inheritance that can never perish, spoil, or fade away kept in heaven for us.

Set your eyes on the hope of what lies ahead forever with Christ. As Peter summarized:

> Therefore, prepare your minds for action; be self-controlled; set your hope fully on the grace to be given you when Jesus Christ is revealed.
>
> 1 Peter 1:13 NIV

It would appear that a genuine revaluation of human life has taken place during the modern period, perhaps because for the first time in history most people don't believe in an afterlife.

"Notes on Optimism,"
Vogue magazine January, 1975

For to me, to live is Christ, and to die is gain.

Philippians 1:27
(APOSTLE PAUL, written from prison
while awaiting trial before Nero)

11

Hope in the Face of Death

The questions of a child are often the fears of an adult—particularly when those questions seem unanswerable.

"Mommy, what happens when I die?"

"Daddy, does everybody go to heaven?"

"Is there really a heaven?"

One mother wrote frankly in a magazine article that when her child asked her questions about dying she was very disturbed. She answered him, "Perhaps you won't die. Perhaps they'll invent something."

This writer said that death and dying were just things people avoided in conversation. She wrote, ". . . Sex was a topic for panel discussions and cocktail-party chatter. We talked about bodies, but nobody talked about death." [102]

A few years ago I was talking with a prominent psychiatrist, a man who counsels hundreds of people in his personal practice. He said, "I'm scared to death of death."

An outstanding Englishman, J. B. Priestley, said, "Mankind is frightened by the mere word 'death' and nowhere more so than in America." [103]

Today there is a growing obsession about death and dying. Dr. Robert Jay Lifton, psychiatrist at Yale University, observed, "Death is the most important question of our time." [104]

Why are psychiatrists, sociologists, scientists, and the clergy "popularizing" the subject of death? There are reasons, foremost among them being the lengthening of the span of life, and the increase in number of the aged in our society. Also, with the advances in medical science come new problems. The dilemma is facing the medical profession now as never before in history: people can be kept biologically alive for a protracted period of time. How long should human life be extended if it is no longer human life?

Dr. Mansell Pattison of the department of psychiatry and hu-

149

man behavior at the University of California said, "We are in the midst of a reevaluation of death in our culture." [105]

Isn't it strange how many lectures, seminars, and workshops have sprung up on the subject of death and dying? There's a marked preoccupation with the subject. *Psychology Today* recently received thirty thousand replies to a questionnaire on death, surpassing the previous record of twenty thousand replies to a questionnaire on sex.[106]

Death never takes a holiday.

DEATH—NOT SEX

Some schools of psychiatric thought of the past have indicated that most of our personal problems can be traced to sexual beginnings, resulting in neurotic disturbances. However, authorities are changing their evaluation today. Dr. Rollo May, along with a growing number of psychotherapists, warns, "Death—not sex— . . . is the basic cause of man's psychic disorders." [107]

Psychotherapists like Dr. May warn that ". . . man's death-defying sexual instincts have shifted from procreation to performance . . . Americans have frantically turned to sexual titillation for deliverance from the anxiety of death." [108]

These observations by prominent people in the field of psychology are important. While many are trying to interpret from man's viewpoint what some of the trends in our society mean, we find that the growing violence of our day is being interpreted in a new light. *Newsweek* observes, ". . . the violence erupting in U.S. cities is fed, many social psychologists now believe, by a desperate need to avoid death." [109]

How does the Hope Book answer this? God's Word is extremely accurate and relevant. It says that Jesus came to ". . . free those who all their lives were held in slavery by their fear of death" (Hebrews 2:15 NIV).

LIVING WITH HOPE

If the psychologists are correct—and the Bible says they are— then the most basic cause of neuroses and psychoses can be solved by the new birth of eternal life. The new birth not only gives us life with the reality of a new self with God's nature in it, but also it gives us life which is everlasting.

From the moment we are born again we receive never-ending life which is God's own kind of life.

This is why Jesus said, " 'I tell you the truth, whoever hears my word and believes him who sent me has eternal life and will not be condemned; he has crossed over from death to life' " (John 5:24 NIV).

Whether we fully realize it or not, our basic overall mental health begins to be improved with the first assurance God's Spirit gives us of immortality.

The Scriptures testify that God receives us "in the hope of eternal life, which God, who cannot lie, promised long ages ago" (Titus 1:2).

God restates the promise of eternal life forty-three times directly and many more times indirectly in the New Testament. This gives believers strong assurance of the essential knowledge we need to deliver us from the subconscious anxiety about the end of life.

Just thinking—wouldn't it be tremendous if every mental-health clinic had these promises of eternal life as a daily part of its therapy? Wouldn't it be revolutionary if these hospital centers were staffed with enough believers to convey this message of hope to so many who seem mentally hopeless?

THE PERILOUS GAMBLE

Jesus made an incredible promise when He said, ". . . I am the resurrection and the life. He who believes in me will live, even though he dies . . ." (John 11:25 NIV).

The person who believes in Jesus should never get over the thrill of his hope of eternal life.

What about the secular man—the one who denies Jesus Christ or ignores Him? He can't relate to the idea of life after death. He has a sense of foreboding about what would happen to him if there really *is* a just Judge of this universe. If—just if, mind you —"those crazy people" who believe the Bible is true are right—

then the nonbeliever might have to face an everlasting conse-
quence for going his own independent way.

So the nonbeliever says, "Let's not think about life after death—
let's just ignore it." Like the mother trying to explain death to her
child, we'll say, "Perhaps you won't die—perhaps they'll invent
something."

Now I realize that the woman's answer was facetious, but the
sad thing was that she didn't have an answer which could quiet
her own heart, let alone her child's.

Take the easy way out—it's more comfortable for secular man
to say there is nothing after death. We only live here and it's all
over when we die. This is why so many college classes and clinics
about death are mushrooming. Since there is no hope after the
grave, death is very ominous. Consequently, these dreadful things
must be rationalized at all costs.

How impossible it is to give comfort at the funeral of an un-
believing person. I've spoken at the funerals where the relatives
and close friends are believers who have been able to not only
bear up under their grief, but also have ministered the joy and
comfort which comes with the sure hope of eternal life. Death is
not the final tragic act of an absurd play we call life—not for a
child of God.

The unbeliever, however, is making a perilous gamble. Look
at the odds. He is betting eternity on the unprovable proposition
that the Bible is a myth and that there is no life after the grave.
Look at both sides. What if believers in Jesus are wrong? The
most we could lose are a few sinful pleasures which in the final
analysis don't make a man truly happy.

But what if the unbeliever is wrong? He will spend forever
paying his gambling debt!

HOPE TREASURE CHEST

Some of the greatest testimonies of the hope of everlasting life
have been shown by people who have experienced eternity's
touch. I remember standing with my arms around two dear
friends who had just lost their oldest son. There was a quiet
assurance in the father's voice when he said, "I know where he is
right now—I know he's with Jesus Christ, the Lord of the universe."

There's a little woman I know, almost ninety years old, who was given up to die by a team of skilled physicians and surgeons. Against all medical odds she was saved for a time from death. As she began to regain her ability to function mentally and talk coherently she began to tell others in the convalescent home of the hope of living forever.

What a hope this is to stabilize our lives in these turbulent days! As we take God's promise of eternal life we are lifted into a new sense of purpose and meaning.

This hope causes us to be able to apply these words of Jesus:

> "Do not store up for yourselves treasures upon earth, where moth and rust destroy, and where thieves break in and steal . . . . for where your treasure is, there your heart will be also."
>
> Matthew 6:19, 21

Since we know where we are going, this hope inspires us to lay aside some things in this life so that we can gain a reward that will be enjoyed forever in the next life.

This is the kind of hope which enables us to deal with our most basic problem—that is, our heart attitude about the things of this world. If the affections of our hearts are correct, the outside of our lives shapes up automatically.

How about it—has your hope of eternal life dimmed? Keep it clearly in front of you! The repercussions are even deeper than you realize.

I love the simple way Corrie ten Boom said it. When her beloved sister, Betsie, died a lingering death in a prison camp, Corrie tried to hold on to the last tangible link, a piece of Betsie's clothing.

When she gave up that threadbare sweater she wrote:

> And so I left behind the last physical tie. It was just as well. It was better. Now what tied me to Betsie was the hope of heaven.[110]

The choking tears of death subside with the promise of eternal life; the gnawing fears of an unknown destiny are erased by the positive assurance of future reward.

What a way to live! With hope in the face of death.

O Lord . . . .
When I consider Thy heavens, the work of Thy fingers,
The moon and the stars, which Thou hast ordained;
What is man, that Thou dost take thought of him?
And the son of man, that Thou dost care for him?
Yet Thou hast made him a little lower than God,
And dost crown him with glory and majesty!

Psalms 8:3–5

KING DAVID of Israel, 1000 B.C.

12

The Light at the End of the Tunnel

In Jerusalem there's a famous tunnel which was constructed by King Hezekiah around 700 B.C. to provide a way to bring water into his besieged city. The tunnel is narrow and winds through a 1,749-foot rocky passageway to the Pool of Siloam.

One time an adventurous group of my friends and I walked through this tunnel, with every second or third person clutching a flashlight. I can remember the eerie feeling I had when my guide disappeared around a bend and I was plunged into complete blackness.

Questions without answers are like a blind journey. Where there's no light at the end of the tunnel, there's no hope.

At the beginning of this book we saw various problems in the lives of several people. Further developments in their lives will show how the light of hope produces wonderful changes.

What a contrast there is between the person who has found hope for life in Jesus Christ—who has been given the capacity for spiritual insight. For the child of God, there's no excuse for not understanding the illuminating answers to the four great questions of life.

We have seen the absurd answers given to the four questions of life by those who represent the logical conclusions of the best of secular philosophy.

Man has gone to extremes to make God unnecessary and push Him out of his mind. In order to embrace the philosophical system of atheism and relativism, man had to reject his own reason.

One of the most destructive donations to mankind has been the elaborate system of thought which has been built from Darwin's Theory of Evolution.

Darwin first taught as a serious scientific idea that man evolved from apes. However, he believed that God created the original materials from which we evolved.

Then the scientists followed who rejected God and swallowed the relative thinking of philosophers like Hegel. They began to

157

teach that God wasn't in the process of origins at all. "God doesn't exist," they believed. Man is simply the highest present form of evolution which started by pure chance.

YOU'RE NOT AN ACCIDENT

Whatever your persuasion may be about this issue, it is no small matter. At stake is your basic self-esteem and the foundation of how you view yourself and fellowman. Remember, whatever you conceive yourself to be, you will act that way.

Personally, I reject any form of the evolutionary theory. I do so on a scientific basis as well as on a biblical one.

If you choose to believe in some form of evolution, that's certainly your privilege. I only insist on two things as a matter of intellectual honesty.

First, that you openly confess you are an evolutionist by faith, not by conclusive evidence.

Second, that you face the ultimate results of your basic belief to your real self-image and your sense of self-worth.

In almost all of our public-school classrooms, evolution is taught not only as fact, but as the only scientific answer to the origin of things. The idea of special Creation, if mentioned at all, is almost always treated with contempt, and those who believe it are ridiculed and made to feel like they are ignorant and backward. They are usually given poor grades.

In California, after years of debate and committee meetings by the Board of Education and their appointed study groups, it was recommended to include the teaching of special Creation as an alternate answer to how the universe began. However, the textbooks are written to express one view and that of Creation is not given as a possibility, nor even an alternative.

I've often wondered how a teacher with an inquiring mind can reconcile evolutionary teaching when not one shred of evidence has ever been established to show how an invertebrate evolved into a vertebrate.

Those who believe this theory seem to have unbounded faith that something will turn up to prove this theory on which they are unwittingly staking their potential as a person—and in many cases, their eternal destiny.

I believe in special Creation—specifically, that God created all things out of pure energy which emanated from Himself. I believe that God in His Triune Person is the uncreated Creator of everything. There is nothing in proven science that can dispute this belief. On the other hand, some of today's greatest scientists believe the same thing.

Dr. Wernher von Braun, the man who was a key individual in masterminding space travel to the moon, says concerning his belief about the origin of man and the universe, "To be forced to believe only one conclusion—that everything in the universe happened by chance—would violate the very objectivity of science itself. Certainly there are those who argue that the universe evolved out of a random process, but what random process could produce the brain of a man or the system of the human eye?"

In response to some questions concerning his views of creation, von Braun wrote a letter to the vice-president of Tustin Institute of Technology in California, and said, "Some people say that science has been unable to prove the existence of God. But, must we really light a candle to see the sun?"

This brilliant scientist concludes: "It is in that same sense of scientific honesty that I endorse the presentation of alternative theories for the origin of the universe, life, and man in the science classroom. It would be an error to overlook the possibility that the universe was planned rather than happening by chance." [111]

Dr. von Braun believes that those who have excluded all other possible theories of how the universe came into being have in effect denied the objectivity of the scientific method and have introduced a very subjective philosophical system in its place.

The Bible says, "By faith we understand that the worlds were prepared by the word of God, so that what is seen was not made out of things which are visible" (Hebrews 11:3).

PURE POWER

Albert Einstein's theory of $E = MC^2$ agrees with this perfectly. God's omnipotent power was expressed in His creative words so that pure energy was harnessed to create the atomic structure of all material things. If we take a motion picture of a hydrogen bomb explosion and run it backward we get some idea of how much power it takes to make a few atoms of hydrogen.

How beautifully simple and yet profound is the statement, "By the word of the LORD the heavens were made, and by the breath of His mouth all their host" (Psalms 33:6).

I have ample evidence that these things are true. The God who testified of these things has worked personally in my life and revealed Himself. The Bible itself has been proven true in my experience because God does what the Bible says He will do. The prophetic Scriptures have been proven in history with a 100 percent accuracy record.

So with this faith and understanding I have no problem of answering "the big four questions" in a way that is life-changing and hope-inspiring.

WHERE DID I COME FROM?

To a Christian who believes God's Word this question is no problem. Instead, the answer gives us a foundation upon which dignity, personal worth, and correct behavior can be built.

In the Genesis account of God's Creation of the heavens and earth it says that God simply spoke the creative words *Let there be* . . . and the world and its wonders came into being.

But when God created man He got personally involved. Not only does it say that God Himself fashioned man's material being out of the various minerals, chemicals, and nutrients of the ground, but that man's immaterial life (that is, his soul and spirit) was breathed into him by God Himself. (*See* Genesis 2:7.)

Concerning this immaterial life which came directly from God's life, God said, ". . . Let Us make man in Our image, according to Our likeness . . ." (Genesis 1:26).

And again it says, "And God created man in His own image, in the image of God He created him; male and female He created them" (Genesis 1:27).

There is no way to believe what the Bible says and also believe that man evolved from animals. Jesus Himself bore witness of this account's historicity, ". . . Have you not read, that He who created them from the beginning MADE THEM MALE AND FEMALE?" (Matthew 19:4). Jesus took this passage as literal history.

If Jesus was wrong, ignorant, or deliberately passing on error, then there is no way of having confidence in Him elsewhere.

Don't fall prey to those men who masquerade as "ministers" and yet say that this whole account is a myth and nonhistorical.

Peter predicted the coming of these false ministers in the last days, "First of all, you must understand that in the last days scoffers will come, scoffing and following their own evil desires . . . . they deliberately forget that long ago by God's word the heavens existed and the earth was formed out of water and with water" (2 Peter 3:3, 5 NIV).

But the simple belief in what God says gives us a deep and dynamic basis of hope. We can begin to form a self-image of one who has great worth to God.

WHO AM I?

To be made in the image of God is to be honored above all other creatures on earth. We are in the image of God in our immaterial being in the sense of having will, intellect, emotion, moral reason and everlasting existence. All of these attributes correspond to God's own being.

In our material being we have a slight similarity to some mammals, but there is a vast difference between our immaterial being and the highest animal because of God's image in us.

What a sense of awe and destiny everyone should feel about himself! Only a believer can really grasp that there's something wonderful about every human being because of God's likeness in him, even though we are marred by the effect of our rebellion against God.

Narramore and Counts in their splendid book *Guilt and Freedom* have a great three-point outline of how the Christian should answer the question, "Who am I?" I am going to borrow from them. They are: "I am very special." "I am deeply fallen." "I am loved." [112]

I'M A SPECIAL PERSON

Listen to the healthy self-esteem that the Shepherd King David had about himself:

> For Thou didst form my inward parts;
> Thou didst weave me in my mother's womb.
> I will give thanks to Thee, for I am fearfully and
>   wonderfully made;
>
> .   .   .   .
>
> My frame was not hidden from Thee,
> When I was made in secret . . . .
> Thine eyes have seen my unformed substance;
> And in Thy book they were all written,
> The days that were ordained *for me,*
> When as yet there was not one of them.
>
> Psalms 139:13-16

David meditated upon the wonder that he, though an imperfect man, was very special to God. God knew all about us before we were ever born. Even our appearance was all written in His book!

This fact should help many of us to accept the way we look. My twin daughters have just begun to show the impact of the very tenacious and unjust standards of the world. They both wish they could change certain things about themselves. Actually, they're both lovely girls (I'm not prejudiced at all). But even if they weren't—so what. We are being too affected today by the cult of the slim, the beautiful, and the athletic. Character hits zero on the recognition scale.

When a person comprehends how special he is because of his unique creation and likeness to God, it just naturally begins to elevate personal worth and, in turn, behavior. We begin to see our fellowman with new eyes of care and compassion.

I'M A FALLEN PERSON

The very fact that man was created in the image of God made it possible for him to rebel. Man wasn't created as an electronic robot, but with freedom of self-determination.

With our intellect we can think, remember, draw logical conclusions, rationalize facts. With our emotions we can feel intensely about something. With our moral reason or conscience we have an independent witness from God for right and wrong.

The conscience worked okay until man rebelled and went his own way. Then in his fallen state, with spiritual life dead and the Holy Spirit gone, man rationalized his conscience so that it is blurred. Yet it still works to some extent in all men.

When man went his own independent way and rejected his relationship with God, he instantly died spiritually. In this spiritual void, man developed a nature of rebellion against God.

Man is not as bad as he could be, but all of us fall short of God's perfect moral character, which disqualifies us from having a relationship with Him.

The Bible says, "Indeed, there is not a righteous man on earth who continually does good and who never sins" (Ecclesiastes 7:20).

> The heart is more deceitful than all else
> And is desperately sick;
> Who can understand it?
>
> Jeremiah 17:9

> All of us like sheep have gone astray,
> Each of us has turned to his own way;
> But the LORD has caused the iniquilty of us all
> To fall on Him [The Messiah Jesus].
>
> Isaiah 53:6

No wonder the Scripture concludes that, ". . . all have sinned and fall short of the glory of God" (Romans 3:23).

The word for *sin* (*chata*) in the root original sense means to miss the target—to fall short of the bull's-eye. Man misses the purpose for which he was created and keeps on falling short of God's moral perfection.

Since God is perfect, the standard must be perfection. God testifies that ". . . whoever keeps the whole law [of God], and yet stumbles at just one point, is guilty of all of it" (James 2:10 NIV).

We must realize that we are fallen, that we still have the

capacity for rebellion because of the old sin nature. As Christians we must remember that the source of sin in our lives is the old sin nature, not the new self which is born of God and holy. That way we can continue to accept the person that we are in Christ and not let sin cause us to hate ourselves.

It's not very good news to dwell upon our fallen condition. If this were the end of the story, it would be tragic. But it isn't, because:

I'M GREATLY LOVED

God continues to love man even in his rebellious condition, even though our sins deeply grieve Him. God loves the whole world of rebellious men. The Bible says, "This is love: not that we loved God, but that he loved us and sent his Son as an atoning sacrifice for our sins" (1 John 4:10 NIV).

Even when we were going our own independent way and hostile toward God, He loved us so much that He sent His only Son to pay our penalty for breaking God's law. God's Son loved us so much that He willingly died in our place so that our debt for sin was paid in full.

God's great love for each one of us should give us a sense of personal worth and value. The more we center on these truths, the more hope springs up in our hearts and crowds out doubt, despair, and self-hate.

It also begins to cause us to want to live for a God who loves us so much. When we begin to see this we accept ourselves in the way God has remade us. Then we can obey the following Scripture, "Dear friends, since God so loved us, we also ought to love one another" (1 John 4:11 NIV).

Having the hope inspired by understanding God's love for us also causes us to be burdened for those without Jesus Christ:

> For Christ's love compels us, because we are convinced that one died for all, and therefore all died. And he died for all that those who live should no longer live for themselves, but for him who died for them and was raised again. So from now on we regard no one from a worldly point of view . . . .
> 2 Corinthians 5:14–16 NIV

We all once looked at others from the viewpoint of the world. What can they do for me? Are they pretty? Are they popular? Are they rich?

But as Paul says above, when we see that God valued every person enough to pay the infinite price of His Son to save them, we can't reject any man. We want to see all men come into Christ's pardon and be born into God's family.

When a person receives Christ's salvation and begins to learn and comprehend the things discussed in this chapter, he begins to be healed of his psychological hang-ups. The Holy Spirit begins to work in the subconscious as well as the conscious mind and build new dignity and sense of destiny into us. True hope springs forth from this.

The man who sees himself as the product of random chance and merely the present highest form of animal has adopted a philosophy which ultimately programs him for despair.

What a contrast with the Christian who has appropriated the truth about himself! He can look with true hope toward the future and enjoy today. In the present time God urges us "to cast all our cares upon Him, for He cares for us." (*See* 1 Peter 5:7.)

WHY AM I HERE?

The Christian has laid out for him a clear purpose and explanation of life.

The chief purpose of man who is lost is to find God and receive the salvation which He freely offers. God has even ordered the circumstances of men's lives so that they will be most likely to reach out to God. The Scriptures say:

> "From one man he made every nation of men, that they should inhabit the whole earth; and he determined the times set for them and the exact places where they should live. God did this so that men would seek him and perhaps reach out for him and find him, though he is not far from each one of us."
>
> Acts 17:26, 27 NIV

Once we come to be forgiven and born into God's family, we are here for several wonderful reasons.

First, we are here to get to know God better. According to the Bible the purpose of eternal life is, " 'Now this is eternal life: that men may know you, the only true God, and Jesus Christ, whom you have sent' " (John 17:3 NIV).

Second, we are here to mature in our faith, "But grow in the grace and knowledge of our Lord and Savior Jesus Christ . . ." (2 Peter 3:18 NIV).

Third, we are here to bear much fruit. " 'You did not choose me, but I chose you to go and bear fruit—fruit that will last . . .' " (John 15:16 NIV).

The *fruit* refers to demonstrating the characteristics of Christ in our life through the Holy Spirit's power, and also to win many men to faith in Christ.

Fourth, we are here to live exemplary lives and to do good: ". . . who [Jesus] gave himself for us to redeem us from all wickedness and to purify for himself a people that are his very own, eager to do what is good" (Titus 2:14 NIV).

Fifth, we are here to enjoy life through our relationship with the Lord: "Rejoice in the Lord always. I will say it again: Rejoice!" (Philippians 4:4 NIV).

The Apostle Paul summed up why we are here as believers in a unique way. He was under arrest in Rome awaiting trial before Nero which he knew could result in his death. Yet he said, "I eagerly expect and hope that I will in no way be ashamed, but will have sufficient courage so that now as always Christ will be exalted in my body, whether by life or by death. For to me, to live is Christ and to die is gain" (Philippians 1:20, 21 NIV).

Paul's reason for living was for Christ to be manifested in him and through him—manifested in him by the Holy Spirit so that his life was constantly occupied with Jesus Christ and His will—manifested through him by the Holy Spirit so that others could see and be affected by the very character of Christ adorning his life. Paul felt that as long as he was resident in his body in this world that it should be used to glorify Christ.

Paul also said something that only a Christian can reasonably say: ". . . to die is gain." This brings us to the fourth question:

WHERE AM I GOING?

". . . to die is gain." To one without Christ, without hope beyond the grave, this statement seems utterly irrational. But Paul could say this because the Lord promises that "to be absent from the body is to be face to face with the Lord." (*See* 2 Corinthians 5:8.)

Paul actually was torn between two strong desires because of his confident hope of life after death. He said, "I am torn between the two: I desire to depart and be with Christ, which is better by far; but it is more necessary for you that I remain in the body" (Philippians 1:23, 24 NIV).

These passages teach us that the instant we die, our real self—the soul and spirit—consciously leaves our bodies and goes to be in an intimate fellowship with the Lord, awaiting the resurrection of our bodies.

For this generation, we may very well be those who are caught up in the twinkling of an eye to meet the Lord in the air and changed from mortal to immortal without going through physical death.

Paul says, however, that whatever way we go to be with the Lord it's better by far. We will experience eternal joy, peace, and fulfillment with Him. Paul was aching from many wounds received in his body while serving the Lord, so he was ready to go where there's no more pain or sorrow.

Listen, Christian, we are going to a very real place where Jesus is already preparing an incredibly beautiful room for each one in His Father's house. (*See* John 14:1–3.)

And that is the ultimate hope.

HAPPY ENDING . . . NEW BEGINNING

Remember our friends in the first chapter? They began to find the hope they so desperately needed when they found the answers in Jesus Christ.

Out of the hope of the new birth comes the new life, new nature and new image which God has promised. Without knowing the biblical answers to the four great questions of life, the answers are seen in the personal application of the way lives change.

Ted, our friend at the tour party, went to Israel with us in a state of mind which can only be described as restless. I remember the way he paced up and down the corridors at the Rome airport, every muscle in his face taut, his attitude as tense as a candidate the night before election.

After a week of traveling to the places of biblical significance, we came to the beautiful morning when we visited the Garden Tomb. The message was on the evidences of the Resurrection, and its meaning to us. When Ted was confronted with the reality of Jesus Christ, he accepted Him as his Lord and Savior at the very spot where many of us believe He died for us.

When we returned home and developed our trip pictures, we saw the startling change in Ted. Before and after the morning at the Garden Tomb illustrated dramatically the results of the new birth.

Richard, the man who was discharged from the army as a schizophrenic, described his hopeless state of mind and then said, "I have been born again; I have felt Christ's presence; I have found the truth and the truth has set me free. Satan almost had me—now that I know about Satan I know who my enemy is. I can't tell you how much my life has changed.

"Miracles have happened left and right; my thinking has cleared up; I'm a new person."

Ted came from mental confusion to a new life. Richard came from extreme mental disturbance to be a new person.

Remember the woman who cried, "Help me!"? What a magnificent answer she received to that cry. She wrote:

One day, one night, I can't say when, I must have been praying and He answered my prayer saying, "I will help you, but you must let Me." I heard the knock on the door then, and whether through exhaustion of fighting a battle alone or whatever I said, "Come in." I said it first softly, then louder and louder until it seemed I was crying, "Come in!" Since that day I feel as though I have a new life. I've found a comforter that I have never known before. It's the most joyous and beautiful experience in my life.

What about the young housewife who was so frustrated with life that she took up TM and astrology? Her life was miserable. There were some parts of her story which were amusing, especially discovering the strange places my books are sold. She wrote:

> At a cousin's wedding my eye caught the title of your book *The Late Great Planet Earth.* Thinking it was science fiction, I readily put 50 cents in the box. By the way, the wedding was being held in the chapel of the University of South Dakota. I saw your book in a book rack out in the hall.
> I soon discovered I was not reading science fiction. You quoted many Scriptures which caused me to purchase a Bible. I had to see for myself.

She went on to tell about meeting many Christians (accidentally!) and beginning to ask questions. One day while at her job she had a note to contact a customer about a problem. When she called she found out he was a minister. She began to ask him questions and then she wrote:

> He quoted Scriptures so fast, I didn't have time to write them down. When he quoted Romans 10:9, I made a decision to ask Christ into my heart. I did so, right then on the phone. Needless to say, my life has changed completely.

These stories could be multiplied by the thousands. From the letters I have received I am constantly thrilled with the way Jesus Christ changes lives and gives radiant hope to all of us who stumble through life's passageways, looking for the light at the end of the tunnel.

We did not follow cleverly invented stories when we told you about the power and coming of our Lord Jesus Christ, but we were eyewitnesses of his majesty.

2 Peter 1:16
(PETER speaks of prophecy)

13

The Ultimate Hope

The interviewer on the TV talk show seemed astounded at some of the statements I had made. He asked me, "Look, if you really believe that the biblical prophecies preparing the world for the Second Coming of Christ are happening right now—if you honestly think that this generation will experience all those catastrophes which will climax in a global nuclear war, then tell me— how can you keep from dropping out in complete despair?"

"This will probably blow your mind," I answered, "but I expect to be evacuated from this planet in a mysterious way before the worst part of this breaks loose."

I can still remember the look on his face. This statement provoked an incredulous response from the interviewer, who was an agnostic. "Who's going to evacuate you? How will it happen? Will you still be alive?"

He probably thought I was crazy, but he was interested enough to ask me just the question I wanted. "What in the world are you talking about?"

It's the *ultimate hope*. As this generation races toward history's darkest hour, it's imperative that we understand this hope.

In *The Late Great Planet Earth* and *There's a New World Coming* I talked about this "evacuation" in some detail. But it's necessary to restate this great "ultimate trip" briefly and then to make some new observations about how this hope can affect our daily lives in a positive, vital, motivating way.

THE TERMINAL GENERATION

It is my unwavering conviction that this is the Terminal Generation. By this I mean that this generation is witnessing the coming together of all the prophetic signs into the exact pattern that Jesus and the other prophets predicted would immediately precede His return.

I believe the Bible teaches that just preceding the last seven years of history before Jesus Christ returns to this earth He is going to mysteriously and secretly snatch out all those who believe in Him personally. First Corinthians 15:51–53 tells us that this event will happen in the "twinkling of an eye." This is in a context which is talking about resurrection. In the Old Testament the believer understood that he would die and be raised bodily back to life again in the resurrection.

But in the New Testament the Apostle Paul introduces what he calls a mystery. It shows for the first time that there would be a generation who would believe in Jesus Christ and would be caught up to meet Him, would be taken from the earth and changed from mortal to immortal without knowing physical death.

Again the Apostle Paul explains in 1 Thessalonians 4:15–18 that the Lord Himself would descend from heaven and that those who are alive at this time would be caught up together to meet Him in the air and would be with Him forever.

Jesus is preparing our place right now. He says there are going to be many mansions in which we will dwell. When He comes in this secret coming He'll take us to be where He is. This event which I'm describing is commonly called by theologians *the Rapture.*

WHEN WILL THE RAPTURE HAPPEN?

There are some who say that the Rapture will occur at the end of the seven-year holocaust, called the *Tribulation,* and that it will happen simultaneously with the Second Coming of Christ, when He comes personally to set up His Kingdom. If that were true it would contradict John 14, because there it says that He is coming to take us to the Father's house.

If the Rapture occurred at the Second Advent, then we would remain (not be taken) with Him on earth as mortals to be a part of the new millennium kingdom which He is going to immediately institute. It would be impossible to be in heaven and on earth at the same time.

Another passage which deals with the Rapture is:

> For our citizenship is in heaven, from which also we eagerly wait for a Savior, the Lord Jesus Christ; who will transform the

body of our humble state into conformity with the body of His glory, by the exertion of the power that He has even to subject all things to Himself.

Philippians 3:20, 21

These wonderful promises show us what should be the focus of our hope. Our citizenship is already in heaven, for once we believe in Jesus we're secured in the family of God as part of His Kingdom. In our hope we should eagerly await our Savior who is going to transform these bodies that see pain and decay to be exactly like His.

Once again, those who say that this event will occur simultaneously with Christ's return to the earth, must reckon with the fact that our bodies will be changed instantly from mortal to immortal and will be transformed into bodies exactly like that of Jesus Christ.

If this is true, there's no way of explaining how there will be mortal believers to repopulate the earth for the thousand-year reign of Christ after His return. This is something which is promised in the prophecies, particularly in the Old Testament. We know from other Scriptures that it is not possible for those who have the immortal, resurrected bodies to have children, and yet there are many times in the Old Testament that refer to this Kingdom as being a time of prolific child-bearing and many other activities that only mortals could do.

These promises establish a great hope to guide and sustain our lives today. Think of it. During this generation, at any moment, Jesus Christ might come back. We might find ourselves with just the average, mundane day—suddenly, the next moment we're face to face with the Lord! We realize that our bodies are different— that we have been transformed into new bodies which will never know sorrow, or sickness, or aging again. We'll look over and see loved ones who have died long ago. There will be a reunion in the sky along with Jesus Christ.

Then we will be taken immediately to be with Him in His Father's house. There the Scriptures say we will go through a judgment where we will be judged according to our works. This is not a judgment of condemnation, but rather to give rewards.

We will be with Jesus Christ while the earth is being judged for its rejection of the Savior.

We are promised that we will be delivered out of the horrible seven-year period that immediately precedes Jesus Christ's personal return to the earth.

Some have said to me, "Why get so excited about the Rapture?" "Why don't you just teach the Gospel and the Christian life?" "After all, won't this teaching cause Christians to drop out and do nothing to help change the world?"

My first reaction is, "How can we neglect a truth that is so often repeated in the New Testament?" On second thought, "Brother, if you don't get excited about the Rapture, then you must not understand what kind of world this is going to be during the Tribulation."

Jesus said about the Tribulation:

> "For then there will be great distress, unequaled from the beginning of the world until now—and never to be equaled again. If those days had not been cut short, no one would survive, but for the sake of the elect those days will be shortened."
>
> Matthew 24:21, 22 NIV

Revelation chapters 6 through 19 amplifies what Jesus meant here. It tells us that more than half of the world's population will die through earthquakes, freak weather, famine, plagues, and a global war. This all happens within the span of seven years, and accelerates toward the latter part.

So excuse me while I get excited at such promises as Revelation 3:10 which says:

> "Because you have kept the word of My perseverance, I also will keep you from the hour of testing, that hour which is about to come upon the whole world, to test those who dwell upon the earth."

This verse doesn't just promise to preserve the believer through the global period of testing, but to take him out of that time of trial! It is a promise of complete deliverance from the earth through the Rapture.

Why? Because its purpose is to test "those who dwell upon the earth." This last clause is repeated frequently in the Book of Revelation and after tracing it out I found that it could only refer to the unbeliever who rejects Jesus Christ and embraces the Antichrist when he appears.

At the end of the seven years when Jesus Christ returns, Revelation 19 speaks of His coming with clouds of his saints—and that's us. We will come back with Him and be co-rulers with Him on the earth which He will set up.

Another great promise about being delivered from the wrath of God in the Tribulation is found in 1 Thessalonians right after a full statement about the Rapture (in 1 Thessalonians 4:14–18). The promise is:

> But since we belong to the day, let us be self-controlled, putting on faith and love as a breastplate, and the hope of salvation as a helmet. For God did not appoint us to suffer wrath but to receive salvation through our Lord Jesus Christ.
>
> 1 Thessalonians 5:8, 9 NIV

The completion of our salvation occurs when Christ appears and gives us our immortal bodies. This is the hope referred to in verse 8 above. This fact is made obvious also in this verse:

> So Christ was sacrificed once to take away the sins of many people; and he will appear a second time, not to bear sin, but to bring salvation to those who are waiting for him.
>
> Hebrews 9:28 NIV

At the moment we believe in Christ we are forgiven all our sins past and future, given eternal life, born spiritually, become a member of God's forever family, given an inheritance that will never fade away. But salvation isn't complete until we receive our new resurrection bodies at Christ's appearance to us in the Rapture.

This is why the Bible says, "Not only so, but we ourselves, who have the firstfruits of the Spirit, groan inwardly as we wait eagerly for our adoption as sons, the redemption of our bodies" (Romans 8:23 NIV).

MOTIVATING FORCE

What hope! Concentrating on what God has promised in the Rapture produces amazing transformations in motivating people to live for Christ. Thousands have received Christ as a result of hearing about the imminence of this event. Many have written or told me that their lives have been turned back to the Lord because of the hope of this message.

Men and women have decided to go into a lifetime ministry because of their desire to reset priorities inspired by this "blessed hope."

When we focus our hope on the promises of the Rapture, the Bible says definite things should result in our lives. There are exhortations, warnings, and comfort associated with the blessed hope. All of these factors have been relevant to every generation since Jesus ascended to heaven because the Rapture is presented as a possibility at any moment.

There are definite signs to precede the Second Coming, but there are no signs specified to precede the Rapture. Believers of all generations of church history could find an inspiring anticipation in the imminent possibility of Christ's coming suddenly and secretly in the air for them.

But today is different. We see the prophetic signs of the pattern of history which precedes the Second Coming, and since we know that the Rapture occurs before that, we must conclude that it is most definitely the general time of the Rapture.

A COMFORTING HOPE

In 1 Thessalonians 4:13–18, the Apostle Paul comforts those who had Christian loved ones who had died. These early believers apparently were perplexed about whether those who are resurrected from the dead would be united with those who are alive at Christ's coming in the Rapture. He assures them that those who are translated from mortality to immortality as they are caught up to meet the Lord in the air will find that their departed loved ones' bodies will have been raised from the dead a split second before them.

What a thrilling event to anticipate!

We will actually find our loved ones who have died in the Lord waiting for us with Jesus in the clouds.

The Lord then promises that together with our loved ones we will be with the Lord Jesus wherever He goes—*forever*.

It's on this basis that the Lord says, "Therefore comfort one another with these words" (v. 18). What a blessed comfort this is!

As I started this chapter I received a call informing me that the lovely teenage daughter of some dear friends had suddenly died. I thought immediately of the comfort that is in this passage and thanked God that the Christian doesn't have to grieve like the nonbeliever who has no hope.

The father of this girl had a statement read at the service which stirred all of us. When I told him that I was writing this book he gave me permission to quote this testimony.

> Today I know the feeling of a father with an aching, broken heart, for the Lord has chosen to take from us one of our most cherished possessions, our daughter, Maureen.
>
> I have spent most of my life attending church and know about the death of our Lord, and how the Father's heart was broken at this separation. Now I know in part the hurt and pain that God suffered for us.
>
> But through all of this I love the Lord. This is the deepest valley of my life, and even with the great hurt and pain and bitter tears, I grasp the hand of the Lord to lead my way, and in the twinkling of an eye we shall see Maureen again. Then there will be no pain, no suffering, and no tears, and we shall be together again forever. Praise and thanks be to Jesus.

Of course we have sorrow and tears. I have certainly shed tears over friends of mine who have died. But the sorrow is because I miss them—it's because of the sudden shock of not having them around to share things with in this life. Yet, when I think about meeting them again at the Rapture and being with them forever, I'm immediately buoyed up in my sorrow.

One of my spiritual sons recently went through one of the most difficult situations that we can be called upon to bear. His younger brother dropped dead alone in his room. When his father came home and found his son, he picked him up in his arms; he suffered a heart attack from the shock and died a few minutes later.

The only way my friend bore this double sorrow was to focus on the hope of the reunion at the Rapture.

FOREVER HOME WITH OUR FOREVER FAMILY

Another great promise of comfort inspired by the Rapture was given by Jesus shortly before His Crucifixion.

> "Do not let your hearts be troubled. Trust in God; trust also in me. There are many rooms in my Father's house; otherwise, I would have told you. I am going there to prepare a place for you. And if I go and prepare a place for you, I will come back and take you to be with me that you also may be where I am."
>
> John 14:1–3 NIV

The Lord gives us a guaranteed hope that He is going to come back for us and take us to a place of incredible beauty, joy, and peace to be with Him forever.

Not only will we see God and live with Him forever, but we will also dwell with our Christian friends and loved ones from this life.

COMFORT FOR OUR BODIES

A nurse came up to me after I'd just spoken on the signs of Christ's return and said, "Hal, will you please come and meet a soldier I brought over from the veterans' hospital? He accepted Christ as His Savior and Lord as a result of my reading *The Late Great Planet Earth* to him. It really took courage for him to come here tonight—he's in great pain because both arms and legs have been amputated. He lost them in Vietnam."

When I walked up to the wheeled stretcher on which he was lying, the young man looked up with a radiant face and said, "Tell me, Hal, will my new body have arms and legs?"

While choking back tears I turned to Philippians 3:20 and 21 and read:

But our citizenship is in heaven. And we eagerly await a Savior from there, the Lord Jesus Christ, who, by the power that enables him to bring everything under his control, will transform our lowly bodies so that they will be like his glorious body.

Philippians 3:20, 21 NIV

"Jim," I said, "your body will be like Jesus Christ's glorious body. We know that His Resurrection body is perfect, so we know that yours will be, too."

His face flooded with beautiful joy as this promise of God gave birth to hope in him.

You may have an aching, aging, or a badly damaged body. Lay hold of this hope and press on with new strength.

This hope was the basis of the great Apostle Paul's strength in enduring all kinds of physical deprivation and torture. Right after speaking of being "hard pressed on every side . . . perplexed . . . persecuted . . . struck down" (v. 8), Paul says, "Therefore we do not lose heart. Though outwardly we are wasting away, yet inwardly we are being renewed day by day. For our light and momentary troubles are achieving for us an eternal glory that far outweighs them all. So we fix our eyes not on what is seen, but on what is unseen. For what is seen is temporary, but what is unseen is eternal" (2 Corinthians 4:16–18 NIV).

Let's also fix our eyes on "what is unseen and eternal." This refers to the things we will experience in our new forever bodies with Christ.

I believe persecution is coming for most believers in this generation. So these promises and the hope they inspire will be worth more than gold then, if not now. Let this hope inspire us ". . . to throw off everything that hinders and the sin that so easily entangles, and let us run wih perseverance the race marked out for us" (Hebrews 12:1 NIV).

DON'T THROW AWAY THE REWARDS

Here's the push God gives to the Hebrew Christians of Judea who were lagging in their hope and faith:

So do not throw away your confidence; it will be richly rewarded. You need to persevere so that when you have done the will of God, you will receive what he has promised. For in just a very little while,

> "He who is coming will come and will not be late.
>   But my righteous one will live by faith.
> And if he shrinks back,
>   I will not be pleased with him."

But we are not of those who shrink back and are destroyed, but of those who believe and are saved.

Hebrews 10:35–39 NIV

The Lord warns that to shrink back in unbelief, even under persecution, is displeasing to Him. He encourages them to direct their thoughts on the imminent possibility of the Messiah's return. These believers had started out well, but had taken their focus off their hope and centered on their persecution. They were about to throw away their eternal rewards.

So I am thankful for that assurance given at the end of the chapter where He says, "But we are not of those who shrink back and are destroyed" (v. 39).

We can "shrink back" far enough to lose rewards, but not so far that we lose salvation.

WHAT ARE YOUR PRIORITIES?

If we really believe in the hope that Christ could appear today and instantly snatch us up to meet Him face-to-face, it should have a dramatic impact on the way we set our priorities and lifestyle.

Good questions for all of us to ask are, "If Jesus came at this moment, would I be embarrassed?"—"Would this day of my life be pleasing to Him?"

We should plan our lives as if we will be here for a full three score and ten years. But we should seek to live each day as if it's the last one we have. Every day that we live in this world is a gift from God anyway and should be viewed that way.

With world events fitting into the precisely predicted pattern for the return of Jesus Christ, how much more should this Terminal Generation take to heart the passages of exhortation in the Bible. If you are a true believer in Jesus, you may never experience physical death. You may be one who will experience the unbelievable thrill of being instantaneously translated from time to eternity, from mortality to immortality, from the trials of this life to eternal glory with Jesus Christ.

THE SECRET: BE CLOTHED WITH JESUS

The Lord exhorts us that "The night is nearly over; the day is almost here . . ." (Romans 13:12 NIV). When the term *night* is used in this way it refers to the present world system which is alien to God's thinking and controlled ultimately by Satan.

When it speaks of *the day almost being here* it refers to the return of Christ to take us into His eternal presence where only righteousness and peace reign and all is in conformity to His will.

The exhortations are based on this hope. The Lord goes on to say, ". . . So let us put aside the deeds of darkness and put on the armor of light. Let us behave decently, as in the daytime, not in orgies and drunkenness, not in sexual immorality and debauchery, not in dissension and jealousy" (Romans 13:12–13 NIV).

The big question is How do we do all this? First, the motivation to live this way should come from having a fervent living focus on the hope of the Rapture's any-moment occurrence.

Second, the next verse gives us the secret of how to appropriate the power. It says, "Rather, clothe yourselves with the Lord Jesus Christ, and do not think about how to gratify the desires of your sinful nature" (Romans 13:14 NIV).

It is very important to precisely translate the verb *clothe yourselves* from the original Greek. It is in the imperative mood, which means that it is a command from the Lord. It is in the aorist tense, which means that it should be done at once. It is in the passive voice, which means that we, the subjects, should receive the action of being clothed.

God's commands are not options. They are not, "You may if you wish, but suit yourself." The exact translation of that verse in Romans is, "I command you, allow yourselves to be clothed at once with the Lord Jesus Christ and stop thinking about how to gratify the desires of your sinful nature."

How do we allow ourselves to be clothed with Christ? First, we count true the fact that we have been so joined into union with Christ that we are already a new creation—not the old person we were.

Second, we make a choice to reject the constant desires that the sinful nature keeps flashing to our renewed mind.

Third, we make our life available to the Holy Spirit and have an attitude of trust that He will produce Christ's character in us. This is promised in Galatians 5:16, 22, 23, "So I say, live by the Spirit, and you will not gratify the desires of your sinful nature" (v. 16 NIV). Plus, ". . . the fruit of the Spirit is love, joy, peace, patience, kindness, goodness, faithfulness, gentleness and self-control. Against such things there is no law" (vs. 22, 23 NIV).

So when we say *no* to our old sinful nature (you know what yours is and I know mine) and then make ourselves available in faith to the Spirit's control, He clothes us with the above fruits which are the very character of Christ. The more we mature, the more these fruits become evident in our lives. The Holy Spirit gives us the power to keep on rejecting our old sinful behavior.

THE LIVING END

Are we unique in our time with all this emphasis on the Rapture? Not really.

The Apostle Peter lived in the first century and faithfully looked for the possibility of the Rapture occurring in his time. He writes:

> The end of all things is near. Therefore be clear-minded and self-controlled so that you can pray. Above all, love each other deeply, because love covers over a multitude of sins. Offer hospitality to one another without grumbling. Each one should use whatever spiritual gift he has received to serve others, faithfully administering God's grace in its various forms. If anyone speaks, he should do it as one speaking the very words of God. If anyone serves, he should do it with the strength God provides, so that in all things God may be praised through Jesus Christ. To him be the glory and the power for ever and ever. Amen.
>
> 1 Peter 4:7–11 NIV

Peter knew the prophecies concerning the Rapture, but even this great apostle didn't have the insight into prophecy that the diligent believer can have today through the Holy Spirit.

In our time we see that current events unlock areas which were hidden from the understanding of the earlier believers.

Today we can really be sure that "the end of all things is near." How necessary it is to be "clear-minded and self-controlled." Our "minds are made clear" as we apply the truths of God's Word through the Holy Spirit's power to this bewildered and mixed-up world.

I'm so grateful that even *self-control* is something that is produced in us by the Holy Spirit as we rely on Him (*see* Galatians 5:22, 23). I don't know about you, but self-control and personal discipline have never been among my natural assets. What there is in me was put there by the Holy Spirit.

LOVE COVERS ALL

After Peter has given us the commands, he offers some beautiful advice: "Above all, love each other deeply, because love covers over a multitude of sins." This is great to practice anytime, but how much more today as individuals and families are experiencing the increasing anxieties of our pressurized and perplexed society.

I know that in our house there's been an ever-greater need to love and accept one another so that the little annoyances we have with each other don't split us apart. My young teenagers are encountering things in school and among their peer group that I never faced until I was in my twenties. I've found that firmness with them must be accompanied with a loving and accepting spirit or they begin to feel rejected.

Love covers a lot of things that are irritating within a family, just because there are contrasting temperaments and backgrounds which place different values on things.

For instance, my wife is the original pack rat. She doesn't like to throw away anything. I'm a person who likes things cleaned out and in order. My motto is: IF YOU DON'T USE IT, EITHER GIVE IT TO SOMEONE, SELL IT, OR BLOW IT UP.

Well, you can imagine the potential conflict that we have over our garage. My wife has it stacked to the ceiling with various "treasures" that she has accumulated from all the junk stores she frequents. So when I try to get the car into the garage, I find that Jan's treasures constantly have a tendency to creep toward the middle from both sides, leaving no room for the car.

One day, as I was surveying the garage and trying to figure out how to squeeze the car in, I recalled this verse. I thought, *Now how can I apply "Love covers a multitude of sins" to this?*

So I went to Jan and said, "You know, honey, I appreciate the fact that you are a very creative person and that you see pieces of junk in the light of what they can become. Our house is filled with priceless pieces that you made into beautiful antiques. So I accept the fact that with this kind of creative temperament comes the necessity of accumulating lots of junk. But will you please try and keep things clear enough for me to keep the car in the garage, because this means a great deal to me."

Immediately the agitation that had been building in me for weeks left. Since then Jan has conscientiously tried to make room for the car.

Love covered a multitude of sins here, because it prevented an argument and produced change.

Again, one of the fruits that the Holy Spirit produces in the one yielded in faith to Him is God's kind of love which doesn't have conditions.

GIFTS ARE TO BE USED FOR OTHERS

How important it is in these end-times to use whatever spiritual gifts God has given us for the benefit of others. A spiritual gift is a God-given ability which God gives us to enable us to serve the body of Christ. We can't earn or deserve them. God in unmerited grace elects to bestow various gifts to each person so that they can function together as a team in God's overall plan.

No one has all the gifts so that we need each other to minister to each other. Whatever your gift is (and we all have at least one) be diligent to use it for the sake of the other brothers and sisters.

KEEP IT PURE

The Apostle John speaks of the hope of the any-moment return of the Lord this way:

> How great is the love the Father has lavished on us, that we should be called children of God! And that is what we are! The reason the world does not know us is that it did not know him. Dear friends, now we are children of God, and what we will be has not yet been made known. But we know that when he appears, we shall be like him, for we shall see him as he is. Everyone who has this hope in him purifies himself, just as he is pure.
>
> 1 John 3:1–3 NIV

As we see our hope of the above becoming brighter, it produces a tremendous motivation to live a life that is progressively conformed to the image of Jesus Christ.

If we don't have this motivation then there's something wrong with our focus. We need to rekindle the fires of our hope of Christ's coming for us!

What a way to live—with the constant excitement that today—TODAY—may be the one which will signal that it's all over but the shouting in His presence!

Keep your hope at an exciting pitch, because the time is really here. He's coming SOON! Live it up to the hilt for Jesus.

I feel like I did when I ran the quarter mile in high school. I'd always save some reserve until I hit the final turn and tore into the homestretch.

We're in the homestretch. Let it all out and drive to the finish tape where Jesus is waiting!

Amen!

Source Notes

Chapter 1

1 *Los Angeles Times,* January 1, 1976.
2 "The Worry Epidemic," *Psychology Today,* August 1975, p. 76.
3 *U.S. News and World Report,* October 13, 1975, p. 39.
4 *Ibid.,* p. 41.
5 *Los Angeles Times,* October 2, 1975.
6 William W. Brickman, "Adolescents and Alcohol Abuse," *Intellect,* December, 1974, p. 165.
6a *Ibid.*

Chapter 2

7 "Equality—American Dream or Nightmare," *U.S. News and World Report,* August 4, 1975, p. 26.
8 Adrienne Koch, *Philosophy for a Time of Crisis* (New York: E. P. Dutton & Co., Inc., 1959), p. 19.
9 Philo N. Buck, Jr., *An Anthology of World Literature* (New York: Macmillan, Inc., 1940), p. 205.
10 Jacques Monod, *Chance and Necessity* (New York: Alfred A. Knopf, Inc., 1971), p. 112.
11 Jean Paul Sartre, *Nausea* (Baltimore, Md.: Penguin Books, Inc., 1965), p. 126.
12 Bertrand Russell, *A Free Man's Worship* (Portland, Maine: Thomas Mosher, 1927), pp. 6, 7.
13 Quoted by Koch in *Philosophy for a Time of Crisis* from Sartre's *Atheistic Existentialism,* p. 250.
14 Albert Camus, *The Rebel* (New York: Alfred A. Knopf, Inc., 1969), p. 23.
14a *Ibid.,* p. 303.
15 Joseph Satin, *The Humanities Handbook* (New York: Holt, Rinehart, and Winston, Inc., 1969), p. 411.
16 Francis Schaeffer, *He Is There and He Is Not Silent* (Wheaton, Ill.: Tyndale House Publishers, 1972), p. 87.
17 W. Cleon Skousen, *The Naked Communist* (Salt Lake City, Utah: The Reviewer, 1967), pp. 8, 17.

18 Book review by Josiah Thompson in Calendar Section, *Los Angeles Times*, August 5, 1973, p. 54.

19 *Ibid.*

20 Satin, *Humanities Handbook*, p. 413.

21 *Ibid.*

22 Walter Kaufman, *Critique of Religion and Philosophy* (New York: Harper & Row, Publishers, 1958), p. 13.

23 *Los Angeles Times,* June 24, 1973, Part 7, p. 1.

Chapter 3

24 Daniel Sylvester, "The Exhilarated Despair of Francis Bacon," *Art News*, May, 1975.

25 *Ibid.*

26 "Raggedy Andy," *Newsweek*, September 15, 1975, p. 67.

27 *Ibid.,* p. 69.

28 "Sex Rock," *Time*, December 29, 1975, p. 39.

29 "Desert Singers," *Time*, August 18, 1975, p. 41.

30 *Ibid.*

31 "The Backstreet Phantom of Rock," *Time*, October 27, 1975, p. 48.

32 Joseph Satin, *The Humanities Handbook* (New York: Holt, Rinehart, and Winston, Inc., 1969), p. 493.

33 *Film Comment*, July–August, 1975.

33a *Film Comment*, September–October, 1975, p. 8.

34 "Low Noon," *Newsweek*, September 15, 1975, p. 76.

35 "Pleading Insanity," *Time*, November 3, 1975, pp. 70, 72.

36 "A New High," *Time*, September 8, 1975, p. 49.

36a *Newsweek*, September 8, 1975, p. 49.

37 "Worldwide Religious News," *Moody Monthly*, November, 1975, p. 8.

38 Louis Raths et al., *Values and Teaching* (Chicago: Merrill Company, Publishers, 1966), pp. 36, 37.

38a Public Information Office, Los Angeles City Schools, September, 1972.

39 Joseph Adelson, "Education," *Fortune*, April, 1975, p. 140.

Chapter 4

40 *Los Angeles Times*, October 25, 1974.

40a "New Rules Would Help Control Foreign Investments in America," *Los Angeles Times*, February 23, 1975, Part V, p. 3.

40b *Los Angeles Times*, October 25, 1974.

41 Brooklyn, N.Y. *Jewish Press*, January 24, 1975.

42 *Los Angeles Times*, May 7, 1975, Part II, p. 7.

43 "Russia No. 1 Arms Supplier to Third World," *Los Angeles Times*, January 1, 1976, Part I-A.

44 *U.S. News and World Report*, November 24, 1975, p. 40.

45 "China Looks for Neighborhood Allies," *Los Angeles Times*, June 30, 1975, p. 1.

46   *Ibid.*, p. 17.

47   *New York Times,* July 26, 1974, p. 3.

47a "Crowded Earth--Billions More Coming, *U.S. News and World Report,*
     October 21, 1974, p. 54.

48   "Famine," *Time* magazine, November 11, 1974, p. 66.

49   From advertisement inserted by the Environmental Fund, Washing-
     ton, D.C., *Wall Street Journal,* December 27, 1974, p. 9.

50   "Forecast: Earthquake," *Time* magazine, September 1, 1975, p. 50.

50a John R. Gribbin and Stephen H. Plagemann, *The Jupiter Effect* (New
     York: Walker and Company, 1974), p. 9.

Chapter 5

51   Otto Freidrich, *Before the Deluge* (New York: Harper & Row, Pub-
     lishers, 1972), p. 342.

52   *Ibid.*, p. 355.

53   *Ibid.*, p. 351.

54   *Ibid.*, p. 390.

55   "Future Shock Is Right Now," *Oakland Tribune* (California), April
     13, 1975, p. 40.

56   Alvin Toffler, *The Eco-Spasm Report* (New York: Bantam Books, Inc.,
     1975), p. 3.

57   "World Government Predicted," Santa Monica (California) *Evening
     Outlook,* November 3, 1975.

58   "Shouldn't Small Nations Get the Bomb?" *Los Angeles Times,* October
     15, 1975, Part II, p. 7.

59   Theodore A. Couloumbis, "Thinking About the Unthinkable," *Intel-
     lect,* September–October, 1975, p. 94.

60   "International Church Body Urges New Order," Santa Monica (Cali-
     fornia) *Evening Outlook,* December 4, 1975, p. 7.

61   Edwin A. Roberts, Jr., "Mainstreams," *National Observer,* November
     1, 1975, p. 13.

Chapter 6

62   "Merv Griffin Show," October 30, 1975.

63   "The TM Craze," *Time* magazine, October 13, 1975, p. 74.

64   May 12, 1974.

64a Denise Denniston and Peter McWilliams, *The TM Book* (Allen Park,
     Michigan: Versemonger Press, 1975), p. 184. (For further informa-
     tion: *TM: Discovering Energy and Overcoming Stress* by Harold H.
     Bloomfield et al., pp. 193–229; "Spiritual Counterfeits Today and
     Christian Response," A Spiritual Counterfeits Project tract; *Newsweek,*
     January 7, 1974, pp. 73–75; *Right On* newspaper, February, 1974,
     Box 4309, Berkeley, California 94704; *Los Angeles Times,* May 12,
     1974; *Time* magazine, October 13, 1975.)

65   Colin Campbell, "Facts on Transcendental Meditation"; "Part 1:

Transcendence Is As American As Ralph Waldo Emerson," *Psychology Today*, April, 1974, p. 37.

66   "TM: Behind Closed Doors," *Right On* newspaper, November, 1975. A project tract of Spiritual Counterfeits Projects, P.I. Box 4308, Berkeley, California 94704.

67   "The TM Craze," *Time* magazine, October 13, 1974, p. 74.

68   *Inauguration of the Dawn of the Age of Enlightenment*, MIU Press Publication, Number G 186, 1975, p. 47.

68a *New Age Journal*, September, 1975, p. 28.

68b *Ibid.*, pp. 32, 34.

69   *Ibid.*, p. 44.

70   "Mad About Moon," *Time* magazine, November 10, 1975, p. 44.

71   *Ibid.*

72   James Sire, "The Newest Intellectual Fashion," *Eternity*, November, 1975, pp. 40, 41.

73   "Don Juan and the Sorcerer's Apprentice," *Time* magazine, March 5, 1973, p. 36.

74   *Ibid.*, p. 38.

75   "Hemispheric Thinker," *Time* magazine, July 8, 1974, pp. 76, 77.

76   "No *Deus Ex Machina*," *Time* magazine, December 8, 1975, p. 57.

77   *Ibid.*, p. 58.

78   Aldous Huxley, *The Doors of Perception* (New York: Harper & Row, Publishers, 1964), p. 65.

79   *Ibid.*, p. 73.

80   "Language and Reality," *Harper's Magazine*, November, 1974, pp. 47, 52.

81   Sire, "The Newest Intellectual Fashion," p. 40.

82   Gary Kessler, "The Occult Today: Why?" *Intellect*, November, 1975, p. 172.

83   Joseph Adelson, "Education," *Fortune* magazine, April, 1975, p. 40.

Chapter 7

84   Viktor E. Frankl, *Man's Search for Meaning* (New York: Simon & Schuster, Inc., 1959).

85   Francis Brown et al., *A Hebrew and English Lexicon of the Old Testament* (London: Oxford University Press, 1957), p. 875.

86   Robert Baker Girdlestone, *Synonyms of the Old Testament* (Grand Rapids, Michigan: Wm. B. Eerdmans Publishing Company, 1948), p. 104.

87   Brown et al., p. 875.

88   *Ibid.*

Chapter 8

89   "Wake Up! Wake Up!" *Reader's Digest*, December, 1975, p. 69.

90   Sergiu Grossu, *The Church in Today's Catacombs* (New Rochelle, New York: Arlington House, Inc., 1975), p. 187.

91   *Ibid.*
92   William S. McBirnie, *The Search for the Twelve Apostles* (Wheaton, Illinois: Tyndale House Publishers, 1973).
93   Marie Gentert King, Editor, *Foxe's Book of Martyrs* (Old Tappan, New Jersey: Spire Books, Fleming H. Revell Company, 1973), p. 16.
93a *Ibid.,* pp. 86–89.
94   *Ibid.,* p. 69.
95   *Ibid.,* p. 171.
96   Brother Andrew with John and Elizabeth Sherrill, *God's Smuggler* (Old Tappan, New Jersey: Spire Books, Fleming H. Revell Company, 1967), p. 185.
97   *Ibid.,* p. 206.
98   Richard Wurmbrand, *The Wurmbrand Letters* (Pomona, California: Cross Publications, 1967), p. 157.
99   "Bishop Says Gays Must Be Accepted," *Los Angeles Times,* February 7, 1976.
100 Josh McDowell, *Evidence That Demands a Verdict* (Arrowhead Springs, California: Campus Crusade for Christ, 1972), p. 50.
100a *Ibid.,* p. 44.

Chapter 9

101 Maxwell Maltz, *Psycho-Cybernetics* (N. Hollywood, California: Wilshire Book Company, 1964), p. 28.

Chapter 10

101a Bruce Narramore and Bill Counts, *Guilt and Freedom* (Irvine, California: Harvest House Publishers, Inc., 1974).

Chapter 11

102 Judith Viorst, "Let's Talk About Death," *Redbook,* June 1973, p. 33.
103 "How America Lives With Death," *Newsweek,* April 6, 1970, p. 81.
104 *Ibid.*
105 "The American Way of Death Is Changing," *Los Angeles Times,* June 7, 1975, p. 1.
106 Larry Edwards, "Reviving the Art of Dying," *Eternity,* February, 1975, p. 11.
107 "How America Lives With Death," *Newsweek,* April 6, 1970, p. 85.
108 *Ibid.*
109 *Ibid.*
110 Corrie ten Boom with John and Elizabeth Sherrill, *The Hiding Place* (Washington Depot, Connecticut: Chosen Books, 1971), p. 199.

Chapter 12

111 Portions of this letter, written August 14, 1972, were reprinted in a committee report to the California State Board of Education, 1973.
112 Narramore and Counts, *Guilt and Freedom,* pp. 44–51.